THE
CATALOG
OF
AMERICAN
COLLECTIBLES

THE
CATALOG
OF
AMERICAN
COLLECTIBLES

CHRISTOPHER PEARCE

MALLARD
PRESS

MALLARD PRESS

An imprint of BDD Promotional
Book Company, Inc.,
666 Fifth Avenue
New York, NY 10103
Mallard Press and its accompanying design and
logo are trademarks of BDD Promotional Book
Company, Inc.

First published in the United States of America
in 1990 by the Mallard Press

ISBN 0-792-45081-7

A QUINTET BOOK

This book was designed and produced by
Quintet Publishing Limited
6 Blundell Street
London N7 9BH

Creative Director: Peter Bridgewater
Art Director: Ian Hunt
Designer: Anna Brook
Project Editor: Sally Harper
Editor: Susan Ward

Typeset in Great Britain by
Central Southern Typesetters, Eastbourne
Manufactured in Hong Kong by
Regent Publishing Services Limited
Printed in Hong Kong by
Kwong Fat Offset Printing Co., Ltd.

ACKNOWLEDGEMENTS
With thanks to Margaret Pearce and to Ian Howes for the photographs in
this book, and to the many collectors who allowed access to their
collections.

CONTENTS

INTRODUCTION

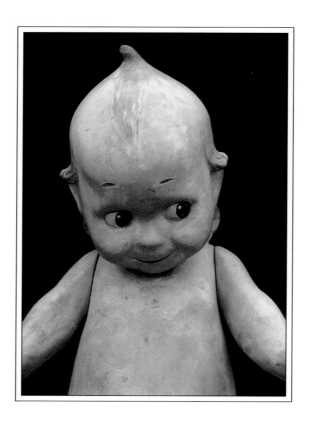

*D*efining a collectible – and a collector!
How the passion starts and the thrill of

pursuit.

ABOVE: *An early Kewpie doll,
now a valued collector's item.*

The enthusiasm for collecting, itself a pastime dating back to ancient civilizations, has increased enormously during the last ten years with the growing popularity of collectibles. Various factors have contributed to this, ranging from the high prices of traditional antiques and the diminishing chances of a find, to an increased awareness of social history and the speed of modern living, which means that even the events of the recent past seem further removed from our present lives than they really are. Nostalgia is there in abundance, but nostalgia in itself doesn't account for the importance of collectibles, which have the power to make historians out of all of us. The quest for knowledge goes hand in hand with the quest for the objects themselves, and nearly every collectible now has its club – which often produces newsletters and magazines – as well as its specialist reference books. These last are listed at the back in the most comprehensive bibliography to date.

To define a collectible is a daunting task – one is tempted to say it is *anything* that people collect – but as that would also embrace old master paintings and property portfolios it is far too vague. Let us say that, in general, for a subject to become collectible, it usually possesses a tangible timeliness, a design that represents an era. In addition a collectible is generally affordable; it is sufficiently common for a collection to be attainable, yet elusive enough for the thrill of the hunt. For many, it is the search which provides as much fun as the collection itself – for not only do junk markets, auctions and swap meets become regular haunts (with vacations and business trips seen as opportunities for pastures new) but the collector becomes a detective, enlisting friends, and relations as extra eyes and ears.

Certain collectibles are excluded from this book for particular reasons. The definition of 'American' has been literally adhered to, so there will be no mention of collectible areas such as Beatles memorabilia, Matchbox or Dinkey toys, Japanese robots and so on. There is a constant re-evaluation of collectibles, and while new subjects appear, other collectibles are elevated to the status of fine art and antiques. American Indian artifacts are an example of this phenomenon. They were originally regarded as curios, progressed to collectibles and are now (at least as far as the best examples are concerned) museum places.

Like the objects of the quest themselves, collectors come in all shapes and forms. Quite often a passion begins with a chance encounter; idle curiosity draws the unsuspecting collector-to-be into the country auction, or to a house clearance sale. This innocent begins the flirtation casually, unaware how the purchase of an iron mangle, a

ABOVE: *This Carnival glass vase is a fine example of machine pressed glass.*

cookie jar, or dusty box of 78 rpm records is about to change his or her life! Passing by a closing-down sale or clearing out an attic can be equally fatal, as can be taking even a polite interest in a friend's collection. For though collectors have the reputation for secrecy and for the jealousy with which they guard their sources, the majority in fact are eager for others to share their enthusiasms, and the triumphs and tribulations of the chase.

This book covers the range of the most common collectibles, and although the occasional rarity is shown, those illustrated are in the main typical examples. Other than in a generalized way, values and prices are not discussed, for these are constantly changing. Collectibles are as much part of our history as the more 'important' items found in museums, and in identifying, researching and preserving them, we not only have the enjoyment of a fascinating hobby, but surely will be also earning the gratitude of future generations.

PHOTOGRAPHIC COLLECTIBLES

*H*istory in black and white: comparing the
charms and values of nudes, post
mortems and documentary pictures.

ABOVE: *Correction officers
posed outside an unidentified
penitentiary, c 1930.*

Collectors of 20th-century objects are the archaelogists of modern times. But instead of excavating ancient burial sites or ruins, they 'dig' in old attics and basements, flea markets and antique shops, to retrieve those bits of the past which constitute their personal passion. Today the historical approach to collecting is of ever-increasing importance – since progress so quickly erodes even the recent past – and collectors, rather than museums or learned institutions, are at the forefront of academic research on these sometimes less-than-scholarly subjects. They can piece together the history of a company – or even a whole industry – that would have otherwise been lost, noting changes in designs, recording details of identifying marks, patents etc. In fact, this and several of the following chapters are about those collectibles which most directly can be seen as a social record. The obvious example must be where the object itself offers a 'self-contained' record, such as a photograph, or old magazine or newspaper.

WHY PHOTOGRAPHS?

Photograph collectors usually direct their efforts toward one of three main areas. Firstly, there are those collectors who are looking for a visual record, a documentary picture that may incorporate another main subject. For instance, those interested in the history and collectibles of the gasoline industry seek old photographs of filling stations. In this instance, age and the details shown in the picture will be the prime concern. The second and largest group consists of enthusiasts whose prime interest is in the history of photography itself.

These collectors often choose to specialize in a particular aspect, such as stereo photographs, daguerreotypes, pictures showing details of fashion or interiors, landscapes or town views. Early studies of nudes, whether genuinely artistic or – more rarely – erotic, are particularly highly prized. Not only were the latter originally produced in small quantities, but they have also had to survive the censorship of intervening generations. You can imagine, for instance, that earlier this century relatives may have been pleased to find a deceased grandfather's Civil War photographs, but less so his secret hoard of erotica! I came across an example of Victorian-style censorship when, prompted by curiosity to discover why a conventional ambrotype of a mother and baby had an off-center matt, I opened it to discover that, underneath the matt, the little boy was completely nude.

A somewhat morbid off-shoot of the second group is the post mortem. Photographic studies of the dead were often made in the last century, and are sometimes found incorporated into mourning

ABOVE: *The documentary photograph is exemplified by these pictures from a series recording a raid on an illicit still during Prohibition. These photographs had originally decorated a law enforcement office.*

jewelry, such as brooches or pendants. Although these sad mementoes, particularly of infants and young children, may appear lurid to modern tastes, they can possess a poignant beauty.

The third area is that of 'fine art' photography. Here the age of the photo is almost irrelevant, more importance being attached to the quality of the picture, and the recognized status of the photographer. Such photographs are more correctly valued as works of art rather than collectibles, and are rarely encountered outside of auction houses and specialist dealers.

AMATEUR PHOTOGRAPHY.

"The sitting, I think, will be a success —
I'll send the proofs in a week, or less."

ABOVE: *From its earliest days, photography was a popular medium for humor. This postcard, published in New York, dates from 1910.*

DAGUERREOTYPES AND COLLODION PLATES

A daguerreotype is the result of a photographic process whereby the image, rather than being printed onto paper via a photographic negative, is made directly onto a sensitized plate of silvered copper. This gives a mirror-like quality to the picture which, when viewed at an angle, still registers a strong image. Some daguerreotypes are tinted. Because the surface was so delicate even the softest brush strokes would have produced scratches, this tinting was achieved by powdered color being spotted onto the appropriate area, and then fixed by being breathed on. A high level of skill was required for this process and, ironically, it was often best supplied by portrait painters who found themselves made redundant by the advent of photography.

Invented by a Frenchman, Louis Daguerre, the eponymous process was first introduced to the United States by Samuel Morse who had visited the Frenchman while in Paris to patent his own invention, the telegraph. Morse was not only an inventor, but also a portrait painter, and had himself conducted unsuccessful experiments in photography. The first daguerreotype in America was taken in 1839 by D.W. Seager. A year later the first American book on photography was printed. Daguerre's agent, Francois Gourand, exhibited examples of the pro-

cess in New York in 1839, and Daguerre followed by opening a school of photography, with Morse as one of his pupils. The next year the school moved to Boston, where its students included Albert Southwood and Josiah Hawes, who were destined to be America's leading daguerreotype photographers. In time, Morse himself opened a school. Among his star pupils was Matthew Brady, whose black-and-white record of the Civil War made him one of the most important of all 19th-century photographers. In contrast, Morse saw his own work only as a means of making money to subsidize his painting.

The 1840s brought a proliferation of photographers; some were simply entrepreneurs cashing in on a new craze, setting up fly-by-night studios and traveling in the company of snake-oil salesmen. But the serious exponents contributed much to photographic history. When the brothers William and Frederick Langenheim opened a studio in Philadelphia, an early client was President Tyler. The two are credited with taking the first advertising photograph, a daguerreotype of 'customers' enjoying a drink at a restaurant.

By the 1850s, the standard of American photography was sufficiently high to attract favorable comments when featured at the 1851 Great Exhibition in London. American daguerreotype plates were produced with a greater surface brilliance and purity than the European variety, which naturally created a better image. The Great Exhibition judges, however, chose to believe that it was the clean air of America that accounted for this clarity, deciding that 'when we consider how important an element of the process is a clear atmosphere, we must be careful not to overrate the superiority of execution which America certainly manifests'.

From that time on, developments moved apace. In the same year, Robert Vance of San Francisco had a New York exhibition of over 300 daguerreotypes, including views of San Francisco, Californian scenery and studies of gold mines and miners, as well as of Pacific coast Indians. S.N. Carvalko accompanied Colonel John C. Fremont's expedition to Utah 1853–54, and managed to take photographs on the peaks of the Rockies, with temperatures down to 30 degrees below zero. E. Brown set off to accompany Commodore Perry's expedition to Japan as official photographer in 1853, also the year of the first news photograph.

Platt D. Babbitt had set up in business on the American side of the Niagara Falls to photograph tourists wanting a unique souvenir. Shortly after there was a tragic boating accident, with one survivor managing to cling to a log jammed between rocks for 18 hours before being finally swept over the Falls. Babbit took several daguerreotypes of this unfortunate, the first time photography had been used to record a 'news' event.

By mid-century, there were some 10,000 dageurreotype photographers, producing about 3,000,000 pictures a year. The daguerreotype continued to be popular in America into the early 1860s, by which time it was almost obsolete in Europe. In appreciating the vast quantity produced, it should be remembered that a proportion would have been inferior, and the survival rate fairly low. In theory, the daguerreotype is a highly permanent photo-

graph if kept airtight and not subjected to heat or strong light. But if the protective glass cover is cracked, or the gummed seal that bonds the plate to the glass defective, and air is allowed onto the surface, oxidization quickly sets in. Restoration of such damaged daguerreotypes should always be tackled by an expert conservationist.

It is not unknown for confusion to exist between the daguerreotype and the ambrotype, particularly as they both are often found in small leather covered 'cases' or, less often, 'union' cases. The daguerreotype can be instantly recognized by its silverized mirror-like surface. The photographic process which produced the ambrotype utilized a sensitized glass – not silver – plate.

Frederick Scott Archer is usually credited with the invention of the ambrotype in about 1850–51, although there are other claimants. The sensitized 'collodion' glass plate had two major advantages: it could be used as a negative, from which paper prints could be made, and secondly, the negative could be treated and then backed with black paper or velvet to appear as a positive, or 'ambrotype'. Though printing off paper negatives already existed, the glass process had greater sensitivity, with drastically reduced exposure times. This last meant that the ambrotype was more suited for portraiture than the daguerreotype, although the latter's silvery magic is generally more attractive to collectors than the more somber ambrotype.

From its earliest days, photography was used as the original inspiration for engravings printed in newspapers and journals, the first attempt at documentary illustration. In 1855 the British photographer Roger Fenton undertook the hazardous task of photographing the Crimea War. The previous year, the War Office had appointed two official

LEFT: *Daguerreotypes and ambrotypes immortalize a family, c 1858. These are typical portraits of the period by an unknown photographer, yet their very ordinariness gives them a poignant charm.*

ABOVE: *This union case is a very good example in crisp condition. The bowl of fruit design was made by the Florence Manufacturing Company.*

photographers, but no example of their work survived. Instead it was Fenton's name which became famous as that of the first photographer to make a comprehensive record of scenes from campaigns and of the utter misery of war. His study of the cannonball-studded 'Valley of Death' bears silent testimony of the barrage that decimated the Charge of the Light Brigade.

In America, Matthew Brady, by then a wealthy portrait photographer, took up the gauntlet. With the moral support of President Lincoln but at a personal expense of some $10,000, he set out to record the American Civil War from the Union point of view. It was Brady who pioneered the almost day-to-day photographing of war. His team included the young Alexander Gardner who later set up on his own. With Timothy O'Sullivan, Gardner continued to cover the war. The two were responsible for both greater output and higher quality than Brady; a particular case in point is O'Sullivan's memorable 'The Harvest of Death', after the battle of Gettysburg. The historical and artistic values of these photographs are immeasurable. They freeze time in a way only photographs can. It was these images, for instance, that enabled the realistic tableaux of the Civil War to be so faithfully recreated in films like *Gone With the Wind* and *The Good, The Bad And The Ugly*. Considering their importance, it now seems incredible that it was only during the 1930s that the National Archives at Washington finally acquired some 6,000 Brady negatives which the US War Department had been storing, all but forgotten. During World War II the Library of Congress acquired a further ten thousand.

Although the most important examples of Civil War photography are of battle scenes, there are also individual daguerreotypes and paper portraits of soldiers. Especially collectible are those which are dated and the subject identified, particularly if connected to an important historical event or campaign.

CARTE-DE-VISITES

These portable likenesses, literally the size of a calling card, made their appearance in the 1850s. Although there are several European claims to its invention, an 1855 magazine article attributed the vogue to America. 'The Yankee man of fashion, it is said does not descend to the prosaic plan of engraving his name on his visiting card, but fills his card case with photographs of himself, which he hands out himself'. These little photographs were soon being produced by the million, their popularity fuelled by the craze for collecting them in special albums. Commercially produced portraits of celebrities could be brought to put alongside family photos, as well as pictures of places – the forerunner of the postcard – and reproductions of works of art. There were several suggestions at the time that these small photographs would be ideal to use on passports, and although not taken up by the authorities, it was adopted by the Chicago and Milwaukee Railway Company in 1861 for season tickets – the first use of the ID photo.

Such was the popularity of the carte-de-visite that between 1864 and 1866 a tax was levied on them of two to five cents, depending on the cost of the picture. The presence of a tax stamp on the back can therefore establish the date.

A particular sort of photograph that also originated in America was the 'tintype'. Although there were earlier practitioners of the process, the photo-sensitized tinned sheet was only patented by Professor Hamilton Smith of Ohio in 1856. Also known as ferrotypes, they continued to be made well into this century. Their relative cheapness meant that they were almost exclusively the provenance of the poorer classes, enjoying their widest popularity as seaside and carnival novelties. Because tintypes could be easily trimmed to size, they were often incorporated into jewelry.

ALBUMS AND CASES

Sometimes collected as an adjunct to photographs but equally a collectible in its own right, the union case is one of those objects which seems to embody the essence of its period. Daguerreotypes were presented in leather covered cases, which were also in vogue for miniature portrait paintings during the immediately pre-photographic period. The first American daguerreotypes and their holders were

described by the *New York Morning Herald* in lyrical terms – 'it is the first time that the rays of sun were ever caught on this continent, and imprisoned in their glory and beauty, in a morocco case with golden clasps'.

The popularity of daguerreotypes created a demand for the cases far in excess of that which miniature painters had required. Soon a case-making industry was established. An early manufacturer was Matthew Brady, who graduated from casemaking to photography. Leather cases became available in different designs and styles, including the 'Eichmeyer', a patented design of 1855 which had a distinctive, rounded look. There was also a vogue for papier mâché cases, often incorporating mother-of-pearl inlays. These specimens and their variants, are generally known as 'miniature' or 'daguerreotype' cases.

In 1854 Samuel Peck patented the 'union' case, a small case made of die-pressed, molded plastic. Although the effect was similar to the molded gutta-percha which was already in use for small items such as jewelry, Peck used a mixture of heated shellac mixed with reinforcing fibers – the first use of thermoplastic. The molded plastic was capable of reproducing fine detail and deep relief, compared with the shallow patterns of the stamped leather cases. A profusion of decorated cases was soon on the market, as well as oval and octagonal-shaped cases. Popular subjects for the case cover included historical scenes – such as the landing of

Columbus, Washington crossing the Delaware and several studies of the Washington monument – images of rural life, and childhood scenes such as 'Mary and her lamb' and children playing with toys (the case would usually contain pictures of children). Religious scenes were also in demand, some of which – such as the angel carrying a child to heaven – remind us of the high mortality rate for children in those times. The Civil War produced designs like the crossed cannons, the camp scene, and 'Union Forever'. (As the photographic supply companies were all in the North, Civil War photographs from the Confederate side are relatively rare.)

The enormous variety of union cases makes them eminently collectible. Unless a case is of great rarity, the condition has to be crisp, without any chips, and able to close tightly. They must be kept in a cool place, away from sunlight, since cases deteriorate with heat. This writer has vivid memories of seeing one at an open-air market warp and crack under the hot sun!

CAMERAS

Despite the importance of Kodak in the history of cameras and photographic equipment, major contributions also came from England, Germany and Japan. It therefore seems that in general, camera collecting has insufficient exclusively American content to bring it within the scope of this book.

ABOVE: *A particularly fine tinted ambrotype study of civil war companions-in-arms. This was most likely to have been taken in a studio tent, set up in camp. The picture is preserved in its original union case.*

EARLY EXPOSITION COLLECTIBLES

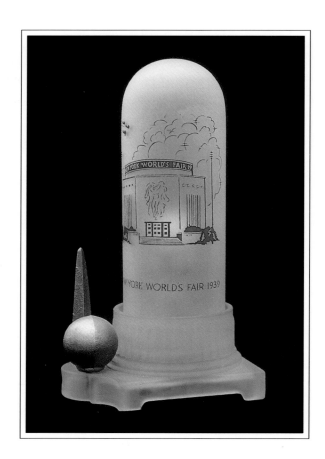

*A*ll's fair for fair lovers in pursuit of salt
and pepper shakers, ashtrays and
lapel pins.

ABOVE: *Souvenir of the 1939
World's Fair in New York.*

ments. The showcase for this was a series of notable American Expositions.

Among the most famous of these industrial fairs were the 1876 Philadelphia Centennial Exhibition, the 1893 Chicago Columbian Exposition, the 1901 Buffalo Pan American Exposition, the 1904 St Louis Louisiana Purchase Exposition, the 1909 Seattle Alaska-Yukon Pacific Exposition and the 1915 San Francisco Panama-Pacific International Exposition. All of these occasions provided souvenirs, postcards and other mementoes which represent the bulk of exhibition collectibles.

While the 18th century brought America national independence and a constitution, and the 19th century the opening up of the country and industrialization, it is this, the 20th century, that has witnessed the emergence of that formidable cliché, the American Way of Life. Many elements of this are reflected in American collectibles, which typify many aspects of uniquely American culture. Shared experiences, such as World War I, Prohibition, Depression and The New Deal all contributed to an inspiring feeling of national identity, aided by the cinema, radio, newspapers and magazines.

Even isolated communities could keep in touch with a wider world by means of the media. Internationally-marketed products, such as Coca-Cola, added to this sense of nationalism, so that both at home and abroad the symbols of America became, not so much the proverbial 'Mom's Apple Pie', but an array of industrial products and creative achieve-

ABOVE LEFT: *Elsie the Borden's cow graces the cover of World's Fair recipes. This item will also appeal to dairy collectors!*

ABOVE RIGHT: *Many World's Fair souvenirs were from exhibitors, such as this pinback button from Gas Wonderland.*

RIGHT: *Molded plastic salt and pepper shakers were a favorite World's Fair souvenir, and although many have survived they are regarded as a classic World's Fair collectible.*

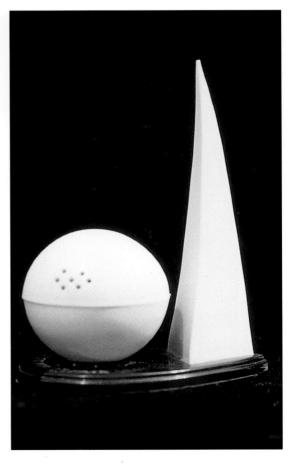

It is, however, the 'modern' exhibitions of the 1930s – the California Pacific Exposition of 1935, the 1936 Cleveland Great Lakes Exposition and, above all, the 1933 Chicago Century of Progress Exposition and the 1939 New York World's Fair – which hold the greatest fascination, for their historical importance as well as for the rich variety of collectibles which they spawned.

The Century of Progress Exposition spurred world recognition of American industrial design and heralded the technological future of a nation which

ABOVE: Brochure featuring both the New York World's Fair and the California Golden Gate Exhibition.

was putting the Depression behind it. The site – consisting of over 400 acres – was filled with buildings that gave a foretaste of the modern architecture for which the United States would become famed in the late 1940s and 1950s. Streamlining was to the fore, and Modernism was emphasized by the world's biggest display of electric lights. The World's Fair of the West, the 1939 San Francisco Golden Gate Exposition, celebrating the completion of the great bridge spanning the entrance to the Bay, was of a similar size. Built on a special Island in the center of San Francisco Bay, this exhibition had as its theme 'Culture and Leisure'. It did much to publicize the Golden State, which at that time was still best known for Hollywood and Orange growing.

No other exhibition – except perhaps Britain's Great Exhibition of 1851, which was after all the grandaddy of all subsequent mega-fairs – has come close to the magic of the 1939 New York World's Fair. It pulled in a total of over sixty million visitors. Since every exhibit offered a profusion of souvenir items, many given away free, and as World's Fair souvenirs were also marketed outside the exhibition, the potential number of collectibles from this source alone is staggering.

Over 25,000 different items, by some 900 licensed manufacturers, featured the famous Trylon and Perisphere, the Henry Dreyfus-designed symbols of the Fair. Articles ranged from a kitchen table with the Trylon/Perisphere design in the fair colors of blue and orange on its white enamel top, to the RCA World's Fair radio, as well as ever-popular

BELOW LEFT: World's Fair souvenir flask.

BELOW RIGHT: This tin bank was a souvenir of the American Can Company's pavilion at the Century of Progress Exhibition, 1934.

salt and pepper shakers, clocks, wall plaques, ashtrays and lapel pins. To assemble a comprehensive collection of Trylon/Perisphere items alone would be a daunting task, and yet they would represent only one aspect of the World's Fair collectibles.

However, volume in itself does not account for the fascination of World's Fair collectibles. Rather the Fair was a landmark event which drew people from far and wide and presaged many of the changes which would confront the nation after World War II. Opening on the 150th anniversary of George Washington's inauguration, the Fair occupied a 1,250-acre site in Queens, New York. An expenditure of $150,000,000 ensured that every aspect of the exhibition was of the highest standard, featuring the work of such respected industrial designers as Raymond Loewy, Donald Desky, Russell Wright, Gilbert Rohde and Walter Dorwin Teague. As well as including educational sections such as communications and business systems, production and distribution, and transportation and community

THIS PAGE: *World's Fair matchbooks would have been taken home by thousands of visitors.*

interests, the exhibition had a high entertainment content. Attractions like Billy Rose's Aquacade – a water spectacular featuring Johnny Weissmuller of Tarzan fame and Eleanor Holm – The Savoy Dance Center with its Harlem Jitterbug Show, and a 200-ft (60 m) parachute jump were among the best attended events. Some of the finest collectibles are from the commercial exhibitors, who backed such arresting contributions as the General Motors' Futurama, the spectacular National Cash Register

ABOVE: Souvenir metal ashtray from the New York World's Fair, 1965.

building, and a massive 14-ton (12.6 tonne) Underwood Typewriter that actually worked, typing on 9 × 12 ft (2.7 × 3.6 m) sheets of paper! To many visitors, however, the overwhelming impression of the Fair was quantity of food, for in addition to the 'five-and-dime' restaurants and Mayflower's two great doughnut restaurants, eateries included The Wonder Bread Bakery,   the Heinz Restaurant and Borden's Dairy World, which issued a book of World's Fair recipes.

COLA
COLLECTIBLES

The joys of finding 'the real thing' in prime
condition, whether it be a Santa Claus
cut-out or a Norman Rockwell calendar.

ABOVE: *This advertisement*
appeared in magazines for
Christmas 1960.

ABOVE, CENTER AND LEFT: Amongst the countless advertising give-aways issued by Coca-Cola, blotters are generally low budget yet highly regarded for their variety and attractiveness.

In the 1930s promotional figurines of the Heinz Tomato, and Elsie, the Borden Cow – with Elmer, her husband – were as familiar to the public as Mickey Mouse. The concept of 'company image' had developed during the century to such a degree that many products had acquired a 'personality' almost transcending the product itself. The prime example of this is Coca-Cola, which was defined by the famous journalist William Allen White in 1938 as 'the sublimated essence of all that America stands for'. The truth of that statement is now almost beyond dispute, endorsed as it was by the American Government during World War II, when it was decided that a constant supply of Coca-Cola was an essential morale-booster for front-line troops. Pop artists, like Robert Rauschenberg and Andy Warhol, further mythologized this symbol.

EASY TO HANDLE · · LESS PARKING SPACE

THIS PAGE : The Coca-Cola blotter took many forms.

Top: *Large-scale cardboard advertising sign, 1945.*

Above: *Score pads such as these dating from 1943 are another example of Coca-Cola inventiveness in finding things to carry the company's name!*

Today, collectors worldwide have made Coca-Cola artefacts, alongside Disney items, *the* American collectibles, with an overseas following almost as avid as the home market. The Coca-Cola cult venerates an enormous pattern of paraphernalia, some of which attract their own specialist following. Advertising posters and bills, toys, buttons and other marketing devices provide a rich lode for the enthusiast. Though old bottles are much sought after, no-one has collected the drink itself for its own sake, save during the notorious 'New Coke' scare of 1985. Then there were reports of people buying up stock of old Coke and cellaring them

like fine wines! There is now no-one who can remember a time before Coca-Cola existed, and as a collectible it has the familiarity of permanence. The traditional flowing script and waisted bottle have achieved worldwide recognition, yet there are so many stages in Coca-Cola history and enough Coke collectibles to ensure that the subject never goes stale.

Excluding rare and extremely valuable 19th-century items, and such specialist items as Coca-Cola chewing gum, Coke collectibles can be broadly divided into the following:

SIGNS AND PLACARDS

The most familiar examples are the outdoor enameled metal and tin signs which were once such a feature of the American landscape. As with all Coca-Cola items there is tremendous variety. The most desirable of the tin signs are those that feature a straight-sided bottle, which indicates that they date before 1915, when the familiar 'hobbleskirt' bottle was introduced. Later pictorial signs showing the bottle, or featuring 'Betty, the Coca-Cola girl', are generally rated more highly than those which are only lettered. Also top of the pops are metal cut-out signs and embossed signs. Although not very old by Coca-Cola standards, as they date from the 1940s and 1950s, the convex 'button' signs are nevertheless popular. Plastic signs, dating from the 1950s onwards, are now being given more attention as a result of the current interest in plastics generally. Illuminated neon signs and glass signs are not particularly common and, of course, have been more vulnerable to damage. Outdoor examples have also been made of wood, masonite and aluminum.

Cut-outs and Festoons

There is a vast array of indoor display signs. Of these, by far the most desirable are cut-out window displays and soda-fountain festoons. Prime examples feature film stars (including Sue Carol, Jean Harlow, Joan Blondell, Lupe Velez and Frances Dee with Gene Raymond), while other sought-after variations are illustrated by Norman Rockwell. A particularly interesting set of cut-outs is the service girls of 1944. These five girls in wartime uniforms, each holding a bottle of Coca-Cola, came either as life-size free-standing cut-outs or as small counter displays. (As with all advertising it must be remembered that war-time restrictions prevented metal from being used.)

LEFT: *This exceptional quality sign of embossed, enameled metal advised motorists that they were approaching a school zone – at the same time publicizing Coca-Cola.*

FAR LEFT: *1940s cardboard advertisement with wood and metal frame.*

A good deal of patriotic material was printed onto paper or cardboard, and Coca-Cola produced various war-related adverts. Another very popular cut-out today is the Coca-Cola Santa Claus. Although Coca-Cola did not actually *invent* Santa, artist Haddan Sunblom's creation came to epitomize the festive old man. He appeared every Christmas from the 1930s to the early 1960s, moving from the restrictions of the cut-out to the wider opportunities of general advertising.

ABOVE: *Die cut card 'snowman' festoon, 1930s.*

LEFT: *Haddon Sundblom created his first Coca-Cola Santa in 1931, and the company's advertising became part of the seasonal scene. This cardboard die-cut display dates from the 1940s.*

Festoons are cut-outs which were intended to be hung above soda-fountain back bars and were popular from the 1920s into the early 1950s. Like all cardboard cut-outs, they were vulnerable to damage, and top examples are expected to not only be in good condition but to also be in the original envelope.

Baseball Cut-outs

The national pastime offered an obvious vehicle for advertising and the results are typical of the times when collectibles overlap, since they are of equal interest to baseball as well as Coca-Cola enthusiasts. The 1950s cut-outs included individual portraits of Phil Rizzuto, Monte Irvin, Roy Campanella, Larry Doby, Bill Bruton and Satcher Paige.

(There have been other Coca-Cola/baseball advertisements, most notably a series which appeared in newspapers between 1911 and 1916.)

In addition to the variety of outdoor and indoor publicity covered thus far, other Coca-Cola items find eager buyers. Among the most interesting and collectible are:

Street Car Signs

These date from between the beginning of this century into the 1920s. They were made to a standard size 28×51cm (11×20.5in) to fit the frames which were permanently mounted on the street cars. Other products too, of course, were advertised, and judging from the surviving Coca-Cola examples, as well as those for Wrigley's Chewing Gum, Old Dutch Cleanser, Fairy Soap and the other major advertisers of this period, the interiors of the cars must have been very colorful.

Movie Stars

The silver screen had enormous influences on ideas of beauty, fashion and social behavior in the interwar period. Even Coca-Cola could not escape its

CALENDARS

From the early days Coca-Cola produced promotion calendars, and specialists deem those pre-dating 1914 to be rare. Such terms are relative, however, for there is an insufficient quality of good condition calendars of virtually any age. The majority of calendars are of the 'pretty lady' type – not pin-ups in the salacious sense – and reflect the changes of style and fashion through the years. A major exception to this theme are the American boy scout calendars by Norman Rockwell.

TRAYS

Coca-Cola serving trays have traditionally been considered the heart of the subject, primarily because they are among the outstanding examples of the art of tin lithography. The trays have been in almost continuous production from the earliest days (1897 is the first known date) to the present,

spell. Die cuts and other advertising vehicles reflected the current obsession with Hollywood. Amongst the personalities portrayed in Coca-Cola advertising were Joan Crawford, Madge Evans, Johnny Weissmuller and Maureen O'Sullivan.

Sports Favorites

Ten hanging cardboard signs were produced in 1947 to commemorate some of the great names in contemporary sporting history. The set encompassed images of such greats as Ty Cobb (baseball), Willie Hoppe (billiards), Red Grange (football), Man O'War (racehorse), Gene Tunney (boxing), Ned Day (bowling), Colonial Lady M (gundog), Bonny Jones (golf), Helene Madison (swimming) and Don Budge (tennis).

Coca-Cola also led the ranks in the run of general pictorial advertising. Some of the most attractive specimens are those from the 1940s, incorporating an art deco-style frame, complete with a relief bottle motif. A large number celebrated aspects of daily life, all of course, featuring Coca-Cola. These pieces of advertising are a real social record, presenting a past America as seen by the world of commerce.

ABOVE: *This subtle 'still life' tray dates from 1957.*

RIGHT: *Although this is a modern (1973) reproduction of the original 1917 tray, it is clearly marked as such and so is considered a legitimate collectible, unlike fake items which collectors consider unacceptable.*

FACING PAGE, ABOVE: *Serving trays represent aspects of the Coca-Cola history as well as being specialist collectibles in their own right. This example dates from 1938.*

FACING PAGE, BELOW: *Royal Crown Cola challenged Coke with this 1940s die-cut card Santa display.*

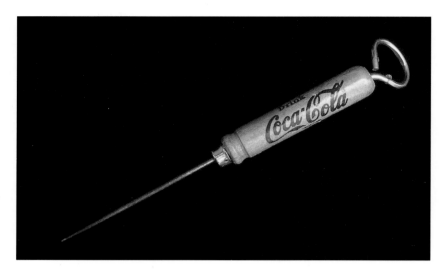

so that through the history of the one item it is possible to chart the history of the company. A drawback tolerated by collectors is that, because they were made for practical use, relatively few have survived in mint condition. Some of the classic early trays have been reproduced and marketed by Coca-Cola, and as such can be considered genuine collectibles, while unauthorized reproductions and fakes cannot.

The smaller change trays existed for a much shorter period, as the more informal 1920s witnessed a decline in change trays generally.

GENERAL ITEMS

Coca-Cola promoted its product through a variety of point-of-sale 'furnishing' items for soda-fountains and stores. Like so much Coke memorabilia, they provide sufficient variety to be specialist subjects in their own right. They can be listed as: clocks, thermometers, lamps, door-push plates, menus, syrup dispensers, bottle coolers and bottle vending machines. For the personal consumer there were school items and educational aids, as well as a copious amount of combs, change purses, playing cards, blotters, notebooks, music and records. In addition, the company has produced numerous

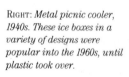

ABOVE: *This combination ice pick and bottle opener dates from the 1930s.*

LEFT: *The round metal button sign, finished in either stone or porcelain enamel paint, proliferated through the 1940s and 1950s, becoming a familiar part of the nation's landscape.*

RIGHT: *Metal picnic cooler, 1940s. These ice boxes in a variety of designs were popular into the 1960s, until plastic took over.*

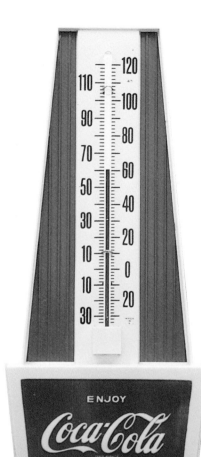

LEFT: *Thermometers in a variety of forms have been a favorite advertising vehicle. This plastic example dates from the 1960s.*

lifesize dummy pony mounted on the sidecar, but also a dummy horse mounted on an automobile chassis, with the 'rider' driving the car. Moxie has its collecting enthusiasts, for the company produced many advertising items, including especially sought-after ones featuring baseball star Ted Williams.

But despite Moxie's eminent collectibility, it remains overshadowed, as are all soft-drink collectibles, by Coca-Cola. Nevertheless, the advertising and publicity materials for these beverages are still highly desirable, with names such as Pepsi-cola, Seven-Up, Dr Pepper, Royal Crown Cola, Hires Root Beer, Mission Orange, Nehri, Whistle and others all having their own following.

BELOW: *Originally there was no standard design for Coca-Cola bottles. The early straight-sided bottle was reproduced for the 75th anniversary commemoration in 1977 by the Huntsville Coca-Cola Bottling Co.*

Coca-Cola toys, including bottling-plant tracks from the 1930s to the present, a toy train by American Flyer dating from the 1920s, marbles, yo-yos (issued at several different periods), puzzles, games – including punchboards – and dolls.

In conclusion, the quantity and variety of Coca-Cola items probably out-number the available sum of some other collectibles several times over. Although Coca-Cola can claim to be the supreme example of a product becoming irreversibly linked with its era, while at the same time successfully evolving, the very enormity of the subject can, for the collector, be a disadvantage. For that reason, it is useful to make a contrast between Coca-Cola and another cult soft-drink collectible, Moxie.

The invention of Moxie pre-dates that of Coca-Cola by a couple of years, and Moxie is regarded as the oldest manufactured soft drink in America. Like Coca-Cola, its origins lay in a patent medicine, a nerve tonic. Its popularity contributed the word 'moxie' to the nation's vocabulary as a slang substitute for 'nervy' or brash. Also like its more well-known rival, it was marketed from the early days with flair and vigor, with advertising images sometimes verging on the surreal. Publicity stunts included not only a motorcycle complete with a

ADVERTISING AND PROMOTIONAL COLLECTIBLES

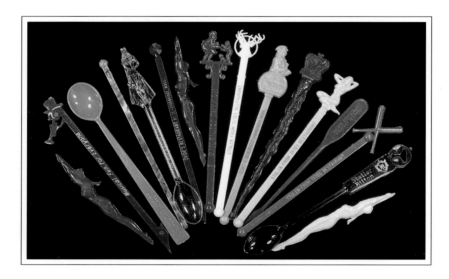

*B*eware of artificially aged reproductions,
and you may find a real treasure of
modern history.

ABOVE: *Swizzle sticks, many of
them bearing an advertising
message, come in a great
variety of shapes.*

Although as a group, soft drinks dominate advertising collectibles, they are nevertheless only part of the story. For not only has the United States led the world in developing a modern advertising industry from as early as the post-Civil War period, but it has also been innovative in marketing and packaging, and in the use of new media – such as signs illuminated by electricity and neon, as well as, later, radio and television. Even these last have left their mark, for though the advertisements themselves are transitory, they engender such things as premiums, and graphic images in magazine ads linked to initial radio or TV themes.

Not only do advertising collectibles encapsulate 'modern' history, the concerns they reflect also range from the parochial to the international. Overlap is always a risk, so that collectors of specialist subjects will also be after advertisements relating to 'their' interest. For instance, a baseball collector will generally put a higher value on a cut-out featuring a baseball star than would a simple collector of advertising memorabilia.

To avoid duplication, the following section will deal with the variety of advertising media rather than with the products themselves, particularly as many collectors base their collection on this system, specializing in porcelain enamel, or matchbooks, for instance. Specific general trends include the fast-increasing prices of good early material – which has the advantage that quality signs are now going to serious collectors rather than the decorators – and the accompanying rise in the quantity of decorator-orientated reproductions. These reproductions, even when made in a traditional way – for example, enamel fixed onto steel, or embossed tin – have a different 'feel' to the real thing. After even a short period of examining originals the novice will be able to spot the difference. However, it must be remembered that 'newness' itself does not necessarily mean that the item is a reproduction, for from time to time genuine discoveries occur of new-old stock, never issued and in pristine condition despite its age. Sometimes there are even sufficient quantities for the market to become temporarily flooded. On the other hand, the collector must be wary, since reproductions can be 'aged' quite convincingly. In the case of enameled advertising signs, it requires only the application of heat, acids and some artistically administered blows – caveat emptor!

Propaganda and political advertising – particularly that concerning civil rights and Black awareness, campaigns such as the 1960s 'legalize cannabis' and other hippie and yippy ideals, women's movements and other special groups issues – are of increasing importance. Since billboards, posters and their varied relations record changes in social

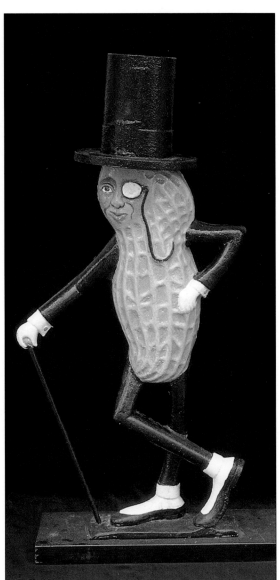

ABOVE AND LEFT: *Large Planters peanut display figure, and small Planters pepper and salt shakers.*

CATHERINE GREY

ELVIA CROX

HATTIE SCHELL

NARRADANSETT
R. I.

TOP: *Kinney Bros issued the actress series of cigarette cards in 1893, featuring 150 famous actresses of the time.*

LEFT: *Pin-up beauty issued with Cockade Cut plug tobacco.*

BELOW LEFT: *'War dance North American Indian' was one of 50 in Kinney Bros' series of national dances, issued in 1889.*

ABOVE RIGHT: *Kinney Bros 'surf beauties' (1889) was a series of 50 cigarette cards featuring bathing belles, each on a different beach. This young lady graces Narragansett beach.*

BELOW RIGHT: *Helen Dauvray in Algerian costume, one of 100 actors and actresses (issued in two series of 50 sets) in 1889.*

HELEN DAUVRAY,
ALGERIAN COSTUME.

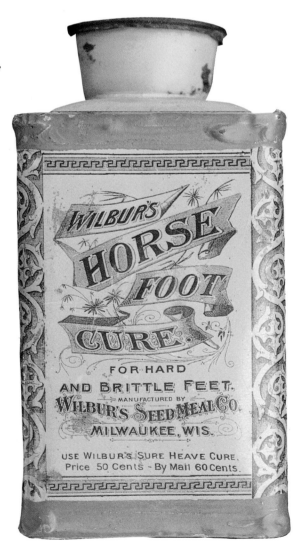

behaviour, further increases in anti-smoking legislation may well mean that the once omnipotent cigarette advertisements become a thing of the past. Already those examples in which brands were endorsed by Hollywood stars such as Ronald Reagan belong to a distant age!

ABOVE LEFT: *Enamel sign for Sweet-Orr workclothes, 1910.*

ABOVE RIGHT: *A splendid metal advertisement dating from the 1880s.*

RIGHT: *Period graphics characterize this tin for Wilburs Horse Foot cure powder; c 1910.*

ENAMEL SIGNS

The enamel sign was the original advertising collectible. Developed at the end of the last century, the technique of firing powdered porcelain onto sheet metal to produce a hard-wearing, weather-resistant, brilliantly colored vitreous enamel finish revolutionized outdoor advertising. In the majority of enamel signs, the colors were applied using a stencil, although later silk-screening was also used to produce finer lines and half-tones. Many signs survived the years to become icons of the industry, their durability emphasizing a common feature: the erstwhile stability of prices. A sign could confidently proclaim an item's cost at five cents, without any fear of inflation making it obsolete! However, the durability of enamel became a disadvantage, together with its high manufacturing costs, so that its use became restricted to such things as safety signs, while new materials, such as plastic, took over the everyday business of promotion.

TIN SIGNS

Although tin signs were once regarded as the poor cousins of enamel specimens, their comparative

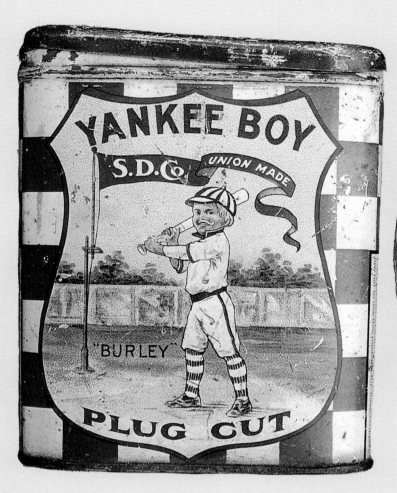

ABOVE: *Good example of a late 19th-century tobacco tin showing typical graphics of the period.*

LEFT: *No opportunity to advertise a product was missed, as exemplified by this 1940s metal door push plate.*

RIGHT: *1950s metal door plate advertising Old Gold cigarettes.*

FACING PAGE, TOP LEFT: *Yankee Boy tobacco tin; note the association between baseball and 'chewing the wad' c 1910.*

FACING PAGE, TOP RIGHT: *Tin sign advertising the New York Metal Ceiling Co., c 1880s.*

FACING PAGE, BELOW: *An early tin, circa 1880s, for Old Gold Cut Virginia Tobacco.*

values have more or less equalized, with collectors now generally prizing age, rarity, condition, quality of graphics and interesting subject matter as being of prime importance. The techniques of litho-printing tin were first developed in Germany in the early 19th century. In those days the technique was used principally in the manufacture of toys and containers, but soon tin signs – either plain or embossed – became an economical alternative to enamel. The tin containers themselves became a useful advertising medium, their decorative quali-ties ensuring that they were preserved long after their original contents had disappeared. Although it is more correctly described as packaging, items such as tin boxes and cans also fit into the world of advertising collectibles. Apart from containers and signs, printed tin in advertising has been used for change or serving trays. (See chapter 3.) While the latter are nearly always associated with food and drink products – especially soft drinks and beers – change trays bear slogans and endorsements for just about everything. There was even a change tray featuring a nude Marilyn Monroe, an offshoot of her calendar posing. One of the most attractive features of the change tray is that it is often a miniature version of an advertisement which was currently appearing on cardboard or paper.

PIN TRAYS

Although these are less common than the larger trays and can be found in other materials, such as china or glass, many pin trays of all types carried advertising, usually for sewing machines, thread and other sewing and haberdashery products.

ABOVE, RIGHT AND FACING PAGE:
Soft drink advertising probably accounts for more tin signs than any other subject.

FAR RIGHT: *Tin sign for Camel cigarettes, 1940.*

ASH TRAYS AND PAPERWEIGHTS

Advertising ashtrays are a popular collectible, having an endless variety of subject matter and style. Materials include: china, glass, cast metal and Bakelite. Some of the most interesting are sculp-tural, incorporating a model of the product. These

ASK FOR

Coleman's

PALE DRY

GINGER ALE

"NOTED FOR ITS FLAVOR"

ENJOY

Grapette

REG. U.S. PAT. OFF.

SODA

IMITATION GRAPE FLAVOR

DRINK

NEHI

REG. U.S. PAT. OFF.

BEVERAGES

ICE NEHI COLD

BEVERAGES

THIS PAGE AND FACING PAGE:
*Enameled tin signs are most
commonly associated with soft
drink advertising.*

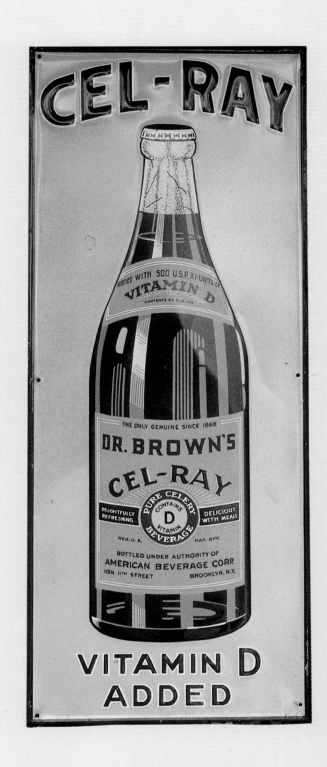

TOP: *Tin advertising change trays c 1910.*

CENTRE, BELOW RIGHT AND FACING PAGE: *Brewery tin trays are much sought after, especially if in desirable mint or very fine condition.*

BELOW LEFT: *A beautiful and well-preserved example of a whiskey advertising tin change tray, c 1900.*

FACING PAGE: *(Top left) this matchbook from the 1930s advertising Henry's Fried Clams claims 'patronizing us is like making love to a widow, you can't overdo it'. (Top center) stylish Art Deco graphics grace this cover advertising Mary Jane's Dining Room, Cabins and Tourist Home, 1930s. (Top right) the Colonial Lunch used the match cover to promote its motto of 'better cooking' in the 1940s. (Center left) quality foods, popular prices – the Brattleboro Restaurant, 1930s. (Center) the El Charro restaurant, Gonzales California, 1930s. (Below left) another example of feature matches, this time 'girlie' pictures hidden within an innocuous cover. (Below center) Howard Johnson's ice cream, 1940s. (Center right) the Art Deco-style New Yorker restaurant, 1940s. (Below right) Monte Proser's copacabana, 1940s.*

characteristics are also true of advertising paperweights.

Other tobacco-related advertising vehicles are cigar cutters and cigarette lighters – frequently used as promotional give-aways – cigarette cards and matchbooks.

MATCHBOOKS

Homage should be paid to the humble matchbook as the first true American collectible. Although previously there had existed collectors of stamps, coins, cheese labels and cigar labels, none of these were uniquely American. The first national club for phillumenists (matchbook collectors) was founded in 1936, but even by then the hobby was well established. Few collectors of any kind could

TOP: *Matchcovers in the 1940s became a major gallery for pin-up art. These were generally stock designs which were personalized for a wide range of commercial advertisers.*

ABOVE: *Wrigleys were early users of matchbook advertising. Their first order was for one billion!*

LEFT: *Advertising war bonds, this World War Two matchbook shows a rear view of Hitler with the message 'strike at the seat of trouble'. An additional novelty is the bomb-shaped matches.*

come close to the legendary Evelyn Hovious, who, from beginning her collection during World War I, amassed over 5,000,000 examples.

The matchbook was invented by Joshua Pusey of Philadelphia, and patented in 1892 – the patent being acquired by the Diamond Match Company. Credit for the first advertising covers must go to the thespians of the Mendelssohn Opera Company of New York who, with no funds for conventional advertising, went to work hand-lettering hundreds of matchbook covers with details of their new production and pasting down photographs of the show's stars. History records that this publicity succeeded in saving the show.

In any event it inspired salesman Henry C. Traute to make up an advertising matchbook for Pabst Brewery. On the strength of this unsolicited sample he received an order for 10,000,000 Pabst matchbooks! Shortly after, Bull Durham Tobacco placed an order for 30,000,000 and a new industry was born. A minor setback occurred when it transpired that the public would not buy them – even at the price of two for one cent. But the indomitable Traute soon solved that problem by persuading tobacconists to give a matchbook free with every purchase. This magic formula proved an instant success, and soon matchbooks were being given

ABOVE: To a collector, bottle caps are no longer throw-away ephemera but precious examples of pop graphics.

BELOW AND FACING PAGE, CENTER: The crimped edge Crown bottle top became a popular soft drink symbol, illustrated here by two large tin signs and a tin menu board.

away all over the place, not just by tobacconists but at restaurants, bars and barbershops, with each specimen extolling the virtue of its respective establishment.

The biggest endorsement of the system was when William Wrigley gave Traute an order for matchbooks to advertise chewing gum. It was a large order – one billion! Over the years, other companies joined the fray, including Atlas, Universal, the Ohio Match Company, Federal, Superior and Monach. Among them they produced matchbooks promoting everything from war bonds to topless massage parlors, from road safety to political campaigns.

Through the years the format has remained much the same, though in 1962 the abrasive striking strip was moved by law from the front to the back. There have been variations – such as where the row of matches themselves make up a design, or extra large books – but the main fascination still lies in the covers, with their range of graphic images from a Vargas pin-up to a Yellow Cab taxi. The written publicity too captures the spirit – and often the idiom – of the period.

The idea of 'free' advertising was also successfully adapted to drinks' coasters and bottle protectors (the paper skirt around the neck of a bottle that stops the liquid from running down the side).

LEFT AND RIGHT: *Bottles proclaim their individuality, relics of the age before standardization and metal cans became the norm. Examples shown here are for Canada Dry and Orange Crush.*

THIS PAGE AND FACING PAGE: *Whiskey bottles enjoyed a boom during the 1970s as a result of a craze for special decorative examples by various distilleries.*

GLASS

Though glass was a popular constituent of signs, ashtrays and paperweights, its biggest use was in glass bottles, beer, whiskey, milk and perfume. As collectibles these fall broadly into the categories of containers for soft drinks. For both soft drinks and beer the bottle was for many years the standard container. Even today variations of some of the 'classic' bottles for Coke, Pepsi and others are still

ABOVE: *Part of the appeal of milk bottles is in the variety of local dairies, most of which have disappeared since 1950s.*

BELOW: *Glass containers displaying Planters' distinctive peanut design.*

FACING PAGE: *This 'baby top' bottle is characterized by the molded face of a baby in the glass.*

on the market, though much under the dominance of canned versions. Having made history by successfully portraying elegant ladies drinking directly from the bottle in the manner of construction workers, the historic power of the bottle is very much a part of the product image.

The breweries pioneered the use of cans in the mid-thirties. Wartime restrictions on the use of metal meant the return of glass, but cans re-emerged after the war. Although beer bottles retain the distinction of greater variety and age, the cans too have their afficianados. Up to prohibition there had been nearly 2,000 breweries, many supplying little more than their local community. Less than a third resumed business after repeal, and thereafter the trend was of merger and takeovers, creating major brands and greater standardization. In addition, breweries have occasionally produced commemorative or 'collectors' bottles. Specials of this sort tend to dominate whiskey collectibles. Jim Beam pioneered the 'special edition' in 1953, and was thereafter followed by a parade of other companies. However the majority of these are more properly described as decanters rather than bottles, since a large number were made in ceramic or heavy lead crystal and take sculptural or figurative forms. After his success with Coke's classic

bottle, Old Forrester commissioned Ramond Loewy to design a special bottle for them, advertising it as the 'decanter sensation'.

MILK BOTTLES

The humble milk bottle is typical of that class of collectibles which sound too ordinary to be the focus of a collection. Yet, basic utility item that it was, it has now gained further appeal as a vanished relic in an age of supermarkets, plastics and no home deliveries. The milk bottle was the creation of the early commercial dairies. Before that time, farmers and dairies would supply milk from churns, the customer providing their own container. The first patented glass bottle appeared in 1880, and soon glass bottles were in use in New York City. By the beginning of this century they were in general use, with thousands of independent dairies selling their milk in customized bottles. Although waxed-paper milk cartons first appeared in the 1920s, glass remained in common use until the 1950s. Then cartons and plastic bottles began the takeover that would eventually all but kill off traditional glass. The variety of collectibles is huge, augmented by the different shapes and sizes of bottles (quarter, half and full pint, third quart, quart, half gallon, and gallon). The bottles were usually clear glass with the name of the dairy embossed or pyroglazed on it. Occasionally a design and/or slogan – 'Fresh to you each morning', for instance – were also included. A popular variation is those with a baby's head design cast in the glass.

   Milk bottle collectors will usually incorporate at least a few examples of bottle caps, cap openers and cappers in their collection. Often dairy items are collectible, and extend the subject from milk bottles to cream separators, milk and butter churns, product advertising, and dairy fittings. The largest commercial dairy conglomerate was Borden's, operating out of Chicago, and its items alone can form the basis of a large collection.

PERFUME BOTTLES

Although commercially produced – as opposed to antique – perfume and display bottles are generally collected, this field is dominated by the Avon bottle. The Avon Company originated with the California Perfume company, founded in 1886. The company pioneered the technique perfected by the Fuller Brush Company, using ladies selling door-to-door. The company became Avon in 1929 and grew to a massive corporation, with over a million 'Avon ladies' internationally. Today all California perfume and many Avon items are collected. Some collectors choose to specialize in the enormous variety of

FACING PAGE: *Ice-cream is a collectors subject in its own right, as well as being included in dairy collections. This exceptionally fine tin sign dates from the 1920s.*

ABOVE: *Original milk bottle tops have usually only survived through having been found unused when dairies have closed down or modernized.*

BELOW: *Milk cartons generally do not have the same nostalgic appeal as glass bottles. However, unusual ones, such as this Hopalong Cassidy design, are of interest.*

TOP RIGHT: *Small dairies capped the bottles by hand, using a capper such as this.*

BELOW RIGHT: *Ice-cream scoops, which come in a variety of patterns, are part of the paraphernalia of ice-cream collectibles.*

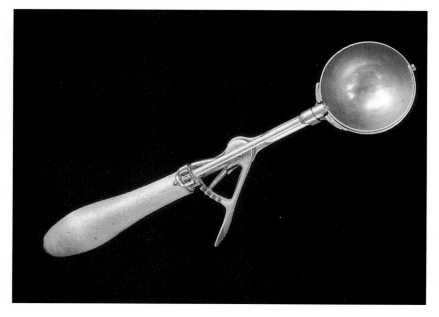

sculptural glass bottles in which Avon packaged men's aftershave, with subjects ranging from a spark plug and a greyhound bus to a snowmobile or a Mack truck.

SWANKYSWIGS

Although Swankyswigs are drinking tumblers, they are also packaging. First introduced during the Depression years of the early 1930s, they originally contained Kraft Cheese. As a marketing device they were a give-away in the same manner as some Depression glass, as there was a free tumbler with each purchase of Kraft Spread. These glasses, with

ABOVE AND BELOW: *Pheasant decanter and Harley Davidson decanter in molded glass are examples of Avon Products' decorative packaging of men's products.*

their brightly painted designs, remained popular until the mid-1970s, with production only discontinued during World War II. There are many designs, some of which were only issued in small quantities.

MIRRORS

Human nature being what it is, few can resist even a casual glance at a mirror, so what a perfect place for an advertising message! Advertising mirrors range from the magnificently etched, embossed and gilded images of opulence especially favored by 19th-century companies to the little, tin-backed vanity mirrors for ladies' handbags, which were popular give-aways from the 1890s to the 1920s.

NEON SIGNS

Neon gas, colored and trapped within a glass tube, twisting and curling into the shape of a name or a device is one of the most dramatic of advertising ploys. Even the simplest sign is capable of making an enormous impact. Neon collecting has been increasing over the last 20 years, with much of the early emphasis not on the product advertised but rather on the intrinsic artistic appeal of the 'neon art' itself. At one time it was an omnipresent part of the American landscape. Indeed, so much was neon synonymous with America, from the gaudy excesses of Times Square or Las Vegas to the lonely highways crossing from the neon-lit signs of theaters and gas stations to the simple scrawl over the soda-fountain, that it is a protected part of American heritage in several historic sites.

The art critic William Wilson described neon as 'the magic wand that gave downtown its boogie-

ABOVE LEFT: *Pepsi-Cola and Seven-Up advertising clocks, 1950s.*

ABOVE RIGHT: *Large advertising mirror for Feen a Mint Laxative, 1920s.*

LEFT: *Dawson's Beer clock, 1940s.*

THIS PAGE AND FACING PAGE: *Early 20th-century advertising mirrors. Those not showing an advertiser's name were salesmen's stock blanks, to be personalised to order.*

LEFT: *Tin soft drink advertising thermometers.*

woogie spirit, etching the edges of buildings, embroidering tapestries of light'. Its presence has seemed so much part of this century that it is surprising how short was its golden age. For neon did not arrive in the United States until 1923 (the world's first neon sign went up in Paris in 1912, two years after its invention), when Earl C. Anthony brought two signs over from France for his Los Angeles Packard showroom. From then until World War II, America went neon mad, erecting advertising signs and clocks all over. In the 1950s neon lost its pre-eminence to illuminated plastic signs and by the 1960s its use had declined to beer advertisements and simple signs. Many of the great neon displays were lost during modernization programs, and civic planning groups were responsible for the enthusiastic removal of vintage signs, in line with the aesthetics of the time. Neon clocks of the late 1930s and 1940s – represented most notably by the products of Neo-Lite Corporation of Ohio – now count as the most sought-after collectibles. At present, while artists and galleries are endeavouring to exploit new possibilities of the medium; collectors and neon conservationists are trying to rescue the remains of America's great neon years.

THERMOMETERS AND CLOCKS

Neon clocks account for only a small aspect of the timepieces used in advertising. Before watches became commonplace, public buildings, stores and offices would have a prominent clock, sometimes mounted on a decorated cast-iron pillar in the

ABOVE: *This assortment of beer labels represents only the tip of the iceberg, considering the variety of beers that have been marketed over the years.*

BELOW: *Whiskey labels are often beautiful examples of commercial printing.*

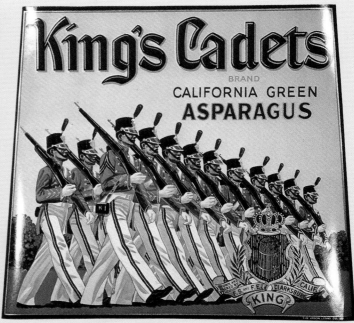

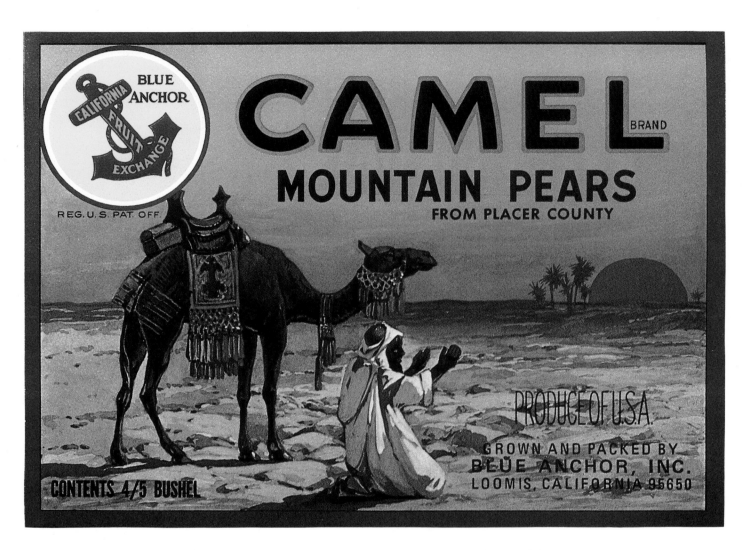

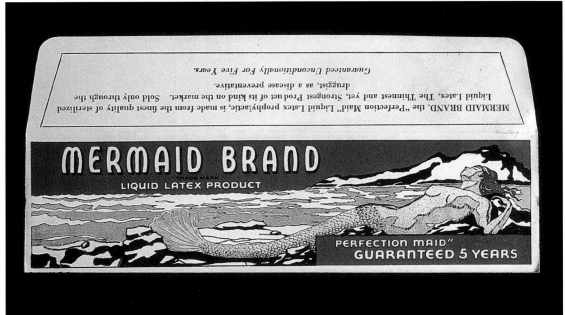

ABOVE AND LEFT: *Vintage condom packs have sufficient appeal to warrant a specialist dealer! They are also of interest to collectors of printed ephemera.*

FACING PAGE, TOP: *Camel Pears label, California, 1930s.*

FACING PAGE, BELOW: *Hustler fruit label, Oregon, 1920s.*

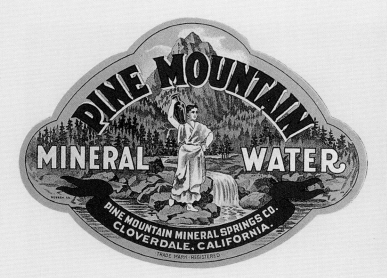

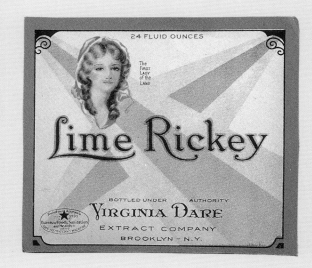

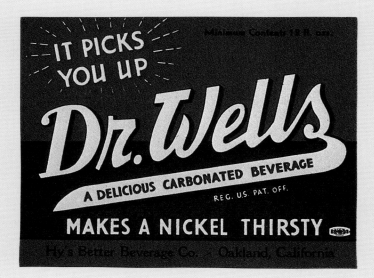

ABOVE AND FACING PAGE, TOP: *Soft drink labels are attractive, low-budget collectibles. As with many drinks, Seven-up was originally marketed as having quasi-medicinal properties.*

RIGHT: *Large paper advertisement for the Victor collar button, 1920s.*

street outside. These clocks often performed the dual purpose as advertising mediums. In the 1880s, clocks were factory-produced, and cheap enough for large companies to supply them to bars, barber-shops, etc as free promotional wares which also provided a public service. An early exponent of such clocks was Coca-Cola, but later virtually every consumer good found its way to a clock face or surround.

Divining the temperature has a similar history to telling the time in relation to advertising gimmicks. Thermometers abound in a variety of materials, from the early cast-iron and wood to plastics. From the last decade of the 19th century, thermometers were often incorporated into a tin, or (less commonly) enamel frame decorated with advertising copy.

PAPER LABELS

Paper labels are some of the most beautiful examples of advertising art, particularly those which come within the confines of 'Fruit Crate Art'. These labels decorated the fruit produce of California

ABOVE: *War-time propaganda items such as these World War Two recruitment posters are valued as graphic art objects as well as for their historical importance.*

RIGHT: *Printed ephemera preserves a moment from history. Against all odds this bag recording a labor dispute has survived from the 1940s.*

and Florida, from the 1880s – when the railroad network allowed for the nationwide transportation of fruit – to the 1950s, when the traditional wooden crate gave way to cardboard cartons. The golden age of the fruit label was from the 1920s to the 1940s, during which time many thousands of different designs were produced. The colorful images were designed to 'sell' the competitive merits of the fruit in the hectic trading of the wholesale warehouses. A multitude of subjects, including landscapes, birds, animals, 'pin-up' girls, trains and Spanish missions are paired with beautiful lettering. The majority of collectors' labels are unused examples which have been found in printers' shops and fruit wholesalers.

POSTERS – PATRIOTIC AND OTHERWISE

Both World Wars provided fertile ground for the imaginative use of the poster. Since the late 1880s and the days of the European artists like Toulouse-Lautrec and Steinlen, the possibilities of the paper hoarding had been exploited on both sides of the

Atlantic to promote products as diverse as: new magazines and books, trains and holiday destinations, food and drink, bicycles and nightclubs. When the government needed to appeal to patriotic sentiment – both for physical and moral support – the poster really came into its own. Recruitment, propaganda and public service announcements blared from walls and barriers; probably the best known of these posters today is the famous World War I example, 'Uncle Sam Needs You!' emblazoned under the old man's staring eyes and pointing finger.

Although advertising was restricted during World War II, many companies engaged in producing

ABOVE: Political campaigns leave behind relics of the fight, such as these bumper stickers of the 1960s.

BELOW: Decals advertising skating rinks are popular with ephemera and sports collectors.

armaments and necessities were allowed to issue patriotic advertisements to keep their name alive until they could resume normal peacetime production. After the war, the art of the poster began an inevitable decline, bested by the aggressive competition of radio and television. Today the majority of posters produced are for records, films and pop concerts – all modish subjects which need to make an immediate impact, since a new event or issue will take its place tomorrow. The old days, when posters appealed to higher emotions or championed claims of consumer trust, are long gone.

Many poster dealers trade through mail order and issue catalogs. The brightness and condition of the poster, as well as its subject matter, are all of paramount importance, and will affect the price accordingly.

TRADE CARDS

These miniature gems of lithography became popular from the 1880s to about World War I. Although trade cards have existed from the 17th century, it was the advent of cheap color printing that popularized the card as an advertising vehicle. Some were available as stock items, which were then personalized by the addition of the advertiser's name and address. But many were custom-produced, the high quality and elaborate artwork representing the epitome of 19th-century commercial graphics. The most attractive cards were collected even in their own time, and scrapbooks of early collectors' collections still sometimes survive.

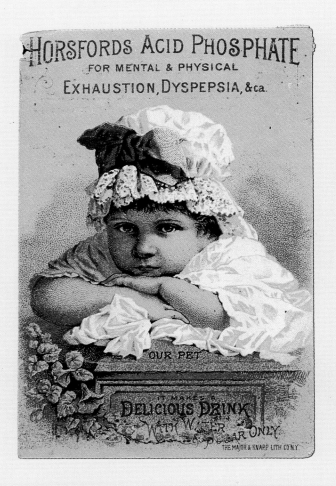

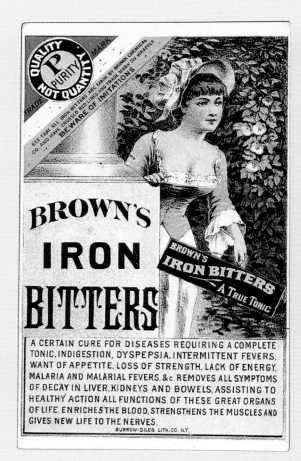

THIS PAGE AND FACING PAGE: *Trade cards: a mirror of their times.*

as well as jackets, caps and various items decorated with a bowling theme.

With over a hundred years of history behind it, and regarded as *the* national sport, it is baseball that has the most impressive pedigree among sport collectibles. Cooperstown, New York, the home of the Baseball Hall of Fame, is both capital and mecca to lovers of the game. The core of the subject is the cult of the Super-Player, who has not only achieved pre-eminence in the game but has taken on the status of a national hero. Everyone knows the names Babe Ruth, Mickey Mantle, Willie Hays, Duke Sneider, Ted Williams, and Joe DiMaggio, for instance. Top items include autographed balls, photos and programs. The stars were also immortalized in portrait figurines made by the Hartland Plastics Company, between 1958 and 1963. These are especially sought-after, as are the special edition portrait postcards by artist Dick Perez, which bear the genuine autograph of the player. On a lower level, there are the vast quantities of 'arcade' cards, dispensed by vending machines, and baseball cards packaged with tobacco, candy and chewing gum. Baseball card collecting is an enormous subject, with some of the most desirable cards now sufficiently valuable to attract forgeries. Originating in the last century, the first cards ('T' cards) came with tobacco. Chewing tobacco has traditionally been linked with baseball since pitchers chewing their 'wad' and spitting before throwing the ball was a classic image of the game.

SPORTSCARDS

The main subjects for collectors are football and baseball, although quite recently interest in bowling collectibles has been growing. The latter include matchbooks and other souvenirs from bowling alleys,

The 1920s saw 'E' cards issued by American Caramel, National Caramel and York Caramel. But from the 1930s to today, gum manufacturers took over. Among the first were Goudey Gum and Gum Inc. After 1945, Bowman Gum and Topps (who eventually took over Bowman) became the main card producers, joined in the 1980s by Fleer and Donruss. Complete sets from various series can be extremely valuable.

In addition to 'star'-related material, baseball collectibles encompass souvenir programs, particularly those for the all-important World Series and All-star games. Programs for games which for one reason or another are important in baseball history are also very desirable, as are yearbooks, which have been produced since the 1940s. 'Special' baseball items include: autographed bats, balls, gloves and mits – which have sometimes been sold to benefit charities – and press-pins, which were first issued to journalists and special guests for World Series' games in 1911. These have the special attraction of being produced in limited quantities.

At present, football collectibles do not generate the same excitement as those for baseball. The first gum cards appeared in 1933 as part of the Goudey Sports Kings set, to be shortly followed by the exclusively football National Chiclets set. After

World War II, both Bowman and Topps issued football cards. Generally speaking, football has not produced the same level of cult hero as baseball, although the same type of material, such as autographed photos, postcards and programs, are available to the enthusiastic collector.

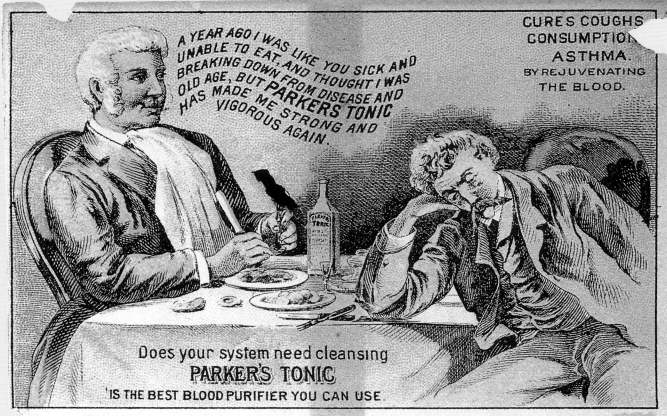

DON'T BUY ANY **MᶜLANE'S PILLS**, WITHOUT THE SIGNATURES Fleming Bros. AND C. MᶜLane.

NEW YORK CITY,
771 BROADWAY, CORNER 9TH ST.

Ladies! The immense crowds that have visited the *GREAT FAIR STORE* every day since the opening, proves that it is a decided success. This is the first time that a store of the kind has been started in New York, and the ladies all acknowledge it is what has long been needed. The few prices that are quoted show what extraordinary bargains are being offered. Ladies' all silk Handkerchiefs, 21 cents, worth 75 cents; Ladies' Silk Clocked Balbriggan Hose, 19 cents, worth 50 cents; Corsets, 24 cents, worth 88 cents; Umbrellas, 27 cents, worth $1. A good article white hemmed Handkerchief, 4 cents; Ladies' and Children's Hose of every description. A complete assortment of Ladies' Underwear, Kid Gloves, Laces, Ribbons, Ties, Notions, Handkerchiefs, Towels, Napkins, Tablecloths, Perfumery, Jewelry, Cutlery, Toilet Articles, Soap, Stationery, Pocket Books, and many other articles for ladies' use. Also, a full line of Gents' Furnishing Goods, at

THE GREAT FAIR STORE,
771 Broadway, cor. 9th St.
☞ *Be careful and look for the number—***771.**

THIS PAGE AND FACING PAGE: *Color and monotone, illustrated and not: a selection of varied trade cards.*

SEE OTHER SIDE

Ladies' Great Fair Store
771 Broadway cor. 9th St. N.Y.

OVER

THIS PAGE AND FACING PAGE: *Trade cards for Yellow Cab, Jessup and Company, Diamond Dyes and Wheeler & Wilson.*

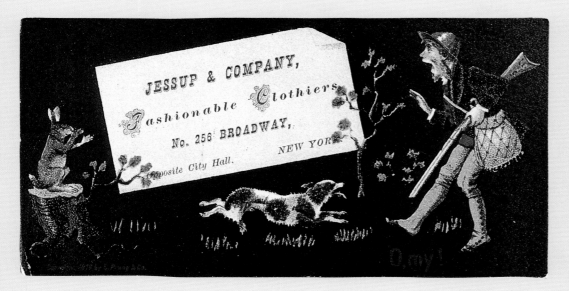

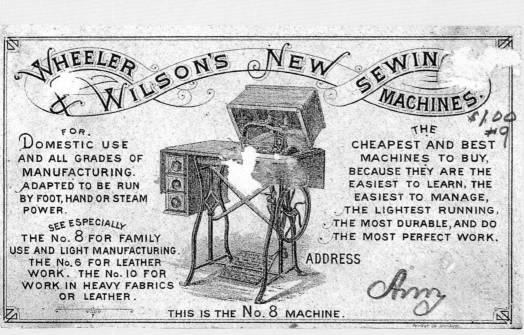

BLACK COLLECTIBLES

NO PLACE LIKE HOME.

The price of past prejudice: an area riddled with dilemmas for the socially aware.

ABOVE: *Produced by T.R. and Co. of New York and probably dating from the 1920s, this photographic postcard of a black family and their house, ironically titled 'There's no place like home', is typically low key but derogatory.*

This chapter continues the broad theme of Chapter I by looking at those collectibles which particularly capture the essence of their time, either as a direct record – as with photography – by evoking a yesterday's triumphs of modernity – such as the great liners, trains and airships – by means of assorted fixtures and fittings.

Every collectible tells its own story from the past, yet it is almost impossible to avoid judging it by present values. For example, a toy which in its day was no more than a cheap item can now seem charming and even well-made, while an example of period advertising can look like a piece of Pop Art. This assessment of items through modern perceptions adds a particular dimension to the area of Black collectibles – one of the most controversial, yet probably the fastest growing, of popular bygones. Although some collectors take the subject into African and Afro-Caribbean art, both of these, together with American pre-Emancipation material, are outside the scope of this book.

A Black collectible, to have any real significance, should represent some aspect of the life and history of Black America. Although items demonstrating the extremes of prejudice or an otherwise derogatory attitude are of great importance for their historical record, an emotive condemnation sometimes accompanies the portrayal of Blacks as cooks and servants or in other servile jobs. Many of these simply reflecting the status quo as it then was, and are not necessarily malicious. Every collector will have to make his or her own decision as to what is or is not acceptable; whether dealing with statuettes of banjo playing 'darkies' or with fictional characters such as Aunt Jemima, or Amos 'n' Andy.

There is certainly one body of opinion which maintains that to be seduced by artefacts commemorating Black personalities from the world of entertainment and sport is simply to further perpetuate a stereotyped image. But the majority of collectors, fully aware of the historical background, see these as legitimate areas for collecting. The question also arises when the collector is presented with figures such as Al Jolson or Amos 'n' Andy, who were actually whites in make-up performing in the role of stereotype Blacks for the amusement of Whites. The case of the dancer Josephine Baker, who captivated Paris, France, with the 'Harlem Image' presents another problem. A beautiful, lithe creature, who was awarded the Medal of the Legion of Honour for her work and was much beloved by the French people, she nevertheless is looked on by many of her more militant brethren as a traitor to Black consciousness. Collecting American furniture carries far fewer pitfalls for the socially aware!

GRAPHICS AND FIGURINES

The biggest single area of Black collectibles is advertising graphics. Black characters were commonly used to promote Southern products such as cotton, and were also deployed – often as children – in visual puns for soap and laundry products. As America became increasingly urbanized through the later 19th century, the South came to represent country values, particularly in cooking. This is typified in the figure of 'Aunt Jemima'. Aunt Jemima Pancake Mix was invented in 1889, when Nancy Green was employed to represent 'Aunt Jemima' at the Chicago Columbian Exposition. The Davis Milling Company endowed the character of Aunt Jemima with a bogus slave background and it was not until the 1960s that the company finally dropped the fiction. Although the 'mammy' was a common stereotype used extensively by other advertisers,

ABOVE: *Although this advertisement for 'Slick Black' hair preparation, by the Valmor Products Company of Chicago c 1940, is primarily concerned with its coloring properties, it also claims to temporarily straighten hair.*

TOP: *Dating from the 1940s, these painted cast concrete figures are yard ornaments. Similar figures as these, but usually of cast iron, were also popular as door stops.*

ABOVE: *These Aunt Jemima and Uncle Mose salt and pepper shakers were molded in plastic by the F and F Mold and Die Company in 1948.*

LEFT: *Painted wood articulated toy figure in the form of a bell hop, c 1930s.*

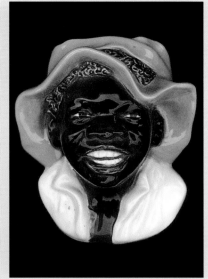

TOP: *Two high quality examples of ceramic bottle stoppers, probably made 1920s–40s.*

ABOVE: *This 1940s birthday card makes a pun on a traditional nursery rhyme.*

LEFT: *This little figure is actually a candle, manufactured c 1955.*

FAR LEFT: *E. Schuberth and Company of New York published a series of 'coon' song albums in 1910–20 featuring such titles as The Larky Little Coon'.*

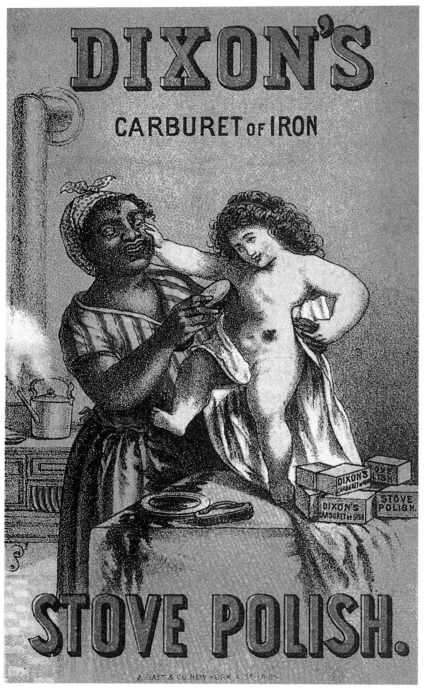

premiums date back to the Chicago Exposition (where Nancy Green demonstrated the mix to over a million visitors). Some of the most popular items include the Aunt Jemima and Uncle Mose plastic salt and pepper shakers made by the F & F Mold and Die Company, a box-top offer in the late 1940s. Similar box-top offers, also through F & F were: syrup pitchers, cookie jars, creamers, sugar bowls and spice holders. Other premiums offered cut-out rag dolls and recipe books. 'Aunt Jemima' items are collected in their own right, as well as forming a subsection of Black Collectibles. Lesser celebrities of the Black advertising pantheon were the 'Gold Dust' (washing powder) twins.

Of greatest interest, however, are those advertisements which actually promoted Black products. Many of these were for cosmetic products, including such dubious items as skin lighteners and hair straighteners. The spread of integration brought greater awareness in advertising, with posters for Pepsi-Cola depicting Black figures, to emphasize the universal appeal of the product.

The history of the civil rights movement, inclusive of Black Pride and Black Power movements, represents a fertile area for the student of black Collectibles. Many items are literary – pamphlets and magazines, including *Jet* and *Ramparts* – as well as posters, lapel buttons and banners. Many items were originally produced in small quantities on a non-commercial basis, making them now very scarce.

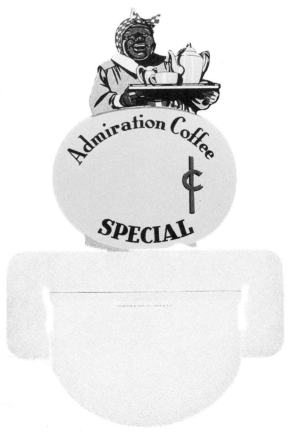

ABOVE: *Printed by A. Gast and Co. of New York and St Louis in the late 1800s, this trade card for Dixons store polish (a black paste used for polishing iron stoves) depicts a 'mammy' playfully applying the polish to a white baby.*

RIGHT: *Though popularized through pancake mixes, the Aunt Jemima figure was adopted for other products.*

FACING PAGE: *This late 19th-century trade card for the Merrick Thread Co. humorously depicts the strength of the cotton.*

as well as featuring in films, 'Aunt Jemima' was the most popular version.

Nancy Green continued to promote the pancake mix until her death in 1923, and was eventually replaced by the actress and singer Edith Wilson, who was hired by Quaker Oats, the new owners of Aunt Jemima mix in the 1950s. By then the Aunt Jemima story had been extended to incorporate 'Uncle Mose', a butler figure, and two children, Diana and Wade. Other Black product personalities who performed the same function as Aunt Jemima were the Cream of Wheat man and the characters fronting the fast-food chain, the Coon Chicken Inns.

In addition to the packaging material, collectibles in this area cover a wide range. Aunt Jemima

Say! what's cookin'?

ABOVE: *A 1940s birthday card with a Black motif.*

BLACK PHOTOGRAPHS

Very early photographs of Black subjects are exceedingly rare. The photo-historians Helmut and Allison Gernsheim relate the curious history of the pioneer daguerreotypist Cyrus Macaire, who passed off underexposed portraits as those of Black people. The earliest examples of genuine photographs date back to the Civil War, and thereafter photographs were taken of Black labourers and domestic servants. From around the 1870s, there is a greater amount of material available, although whether the photographs were posed in the studio of Black photographers is unknown.

Photographic postcards depicting Black subjects also date from this period, the most common type depicting 'scenes from the South': workers in the fields, cooking at their cabins, plucking chickens and other ordinary tasks. There were also 'humorous' postcards, a genre which was popular until World War II. Though more usually illustrative, photographic examples also occur. They almost invariably feature Black stereotypes, often grossly caricatured. Many of these are not only racist but also seek to make fun of poverty.

Other pictorial records from the last century include illustrations from magazines, such as *Harper's Weekly*, and songsheets of 'blackface' white musicians, such as those of the Christy Minstrels. The figure of the 'blackface' minstrel is commonly found not only in America but also in Europe, and predated the celebrity of real Black musicians, who did not come into their own until the early days of barroom jazz.

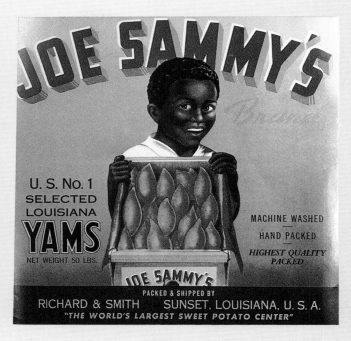

TOP LEFT AND BOTTOM: *Fruit labels dating from the 1930s featuring Black figures.*

TOP RIGHT AND CENTER: *Note the pun on 'black' grapes for 'Uncle Joe' and 'small black' (both from California), and the association of ideas to* promote Joe Sammy's yams from Louisiana and Dixie Boy grapefruit from Florida.

MAIN STREET COLLECTIBLES

*C*apturing fragments of a bygone era filled
with stained-glass barber's poles, trolley
car diners and 'candy store registers'.

ABOVE: *The 1940s and 1950s
saw the proliferation of
modern architect designed
filling stations. This model is
part of the Plasticville range.*

Turning the pages of old newspapers and magazines makes one realize how much the pace of everyday life has altered, even during recent times. While there are still survivors, especially in small towns – the old-fashioned barbershop, diner or 'five-and-dime' – in most cases our townscapes have irretrievably changed.

GASOLINE STATIONS

A case in point is that of the once-familiar traditional gasoline station. Although pioneer motorists could buy their fuel in cans from farm stores and hardware depots, it was not until the advent of the 'filling station' early in this century that a driver could fill his machine directly. In 1905 the Automobile Gasoline Company of St Louis opened the first drive-in filling station. Although this used a homemade gas pump, the inventor Sylvanus Bowser had already the same year produced the forerunner of the modern pump, the Bowser self-measuring gasoline storage pump. A year later John Tokheim invented the Tokheim Dome oil pump, which was the first visible-cylinder pump. In 1913 the first truly modern filling station opened in Pittsburg PA.

Although there were subsequent improvements

ABOVE: This original photo captures the spirit of the wayside gas station, once a familiar part of the rural landscape, c 1930s.

in pump technology – most particularly in the 1933 Wayne computing pump, which showed the cost as well as the quantity of fuel being dispensed – the Pittsburg venture was the cue for the opening of thousands of stations, which soon became familiar parts of the landscape. But today both the rural 'Mom and Pop' stations, which still conjure up images of Bonnie and Clyde, and the high-tech sophisticates of the Art Deco period, have all but disappeared, as gasoline, oil, tires and parts are increasingly sold at shopping centers. Meanwhile self-service has rendered the pump jockey an endangered species.

In the golden age of the 1930s to the 1950s, huge filling stations provided an army of attendants who administered to the needs of the car, while route maps, mileage calculators, give-aways and calendars, were all part of the service. Today all these are gasoline collectibles, together with the pumps and pump globes, air dispensers and gasoline, oil and tire advertisements. Photographs and postcards depicting filling stations – particularly where the location and date are identifiable and the detail is good – are also highly collectible.

In many cases, it is the collectors who have taken on the responsibility of saving much of the local heritage. Other places which – like the filling station – once seemed the quintessence of America, and were under threat of destruction, include the traditional barbershop, the country store and the diner.

The romance of the great American diner began life in 1887, with the first walk-in mobile lunch wagon, the invention of Samuel Jones. From this grew a whole generation of moving eateries which proliferated until halted in the early days of this century when town councils began to enforce restrictions. To circumvent local laws on operating hours, wagons were parked with their wheels boxed in or removed, becoming static restaurants that could, and often did, trade round the clock. Their intimate scale and informality made them popular pit stops, and they enjoyed a respectable reputation for their food, coffee and cleanliness. Usually run by the owner, each diner had its own personality.

By the 1890s this enviable reputation was tarnished by a new generation of 'low life' diners, many

BELOW: *A supreme example of litho metal advertising, this tire advertisement from about 1910 has the flavour of the early days of motoring.*

of which were converted trolley cars. But these often dilapidated and seedy establishments were usurped by the custom-built diners introduced by the 'Diner King' P.J. Tierney, who introduced such conveniences as electricity, ventilation and inside toilets. The diners of Tierney and rival manufacturers set the standard from the 1920s to the 1950s. The majority were factory-built and then delivered to site, although the late 1930s saw the increase of larger diners actually built on site. Diner collectibles include photos and postcards, signs, menu holders, malted milk mixers and stools.

The traditional diner began to suffer in the late 1940s and early 1950s as faster and bigger roads passed them by, while those situated in towns and cities suffered as their custom moved into the suburbs. The new look 'fast food' was heralded by the first drive-in McDonalds, opened in 1955. Planning restrictions and greater sophistication have eroded much of the brashness of the first generation of these fast-food establishments. Collectibles from the era include the premiums issued by companies like: McDonalds, Big Boy, Burger King, Howard Johnson's, Wendy's and Kentucky Fried Chicken, as well as menus, take-out boxes and counter staff uniform items – such as hats, buttons, etc.

BARBERS AND BLADES

Progress has also virtually killed off that unique male sanctuary, the barbershop. Varying from the opulent, marble and mahogany room found in grand hotels and clubs, to the humble street-corner business, the barbershop was a social center, where politics, sports and gossip were discussed during the ritual of haircut and shave. Originally, the barber had also served the community as a surgeon of sorts, a fact which his traditional red-striped pole once advertised. Early American barbers' poles, usually of turned wood with a painted design, are very scarce. In the 19th century they were replaced by illuminated signs, some of which were freestanding on the pavement outside the establishment. These disappeared during urban modernization because they were considered an obstruction. The wall-mounted pole survived, however, although the earlier milk glass and stained-glass affairs from the turn of the century gave way eventually to plastic.

Originally the barber's chair was wood – as exemplified by the magnificent examples by Koken, carved and sumptuously upholstered. These were usurped by the classic vitreous enamel and nickel-plated hydraulic contraptions which gave the barber the freedom to tilt, swivel, raise or lower his client at will. The barber was the maestro of the straight

razor and, even after 'King Gillette' had revolutionized shaving in the 1890s with the safety razor, many men accustomed to the professional's deft touch, continued to patronize the barbershop.

The razor itself would have been either imported from England or Germany, or American-made by such companies as H. Boker and Company, the Garland Cutlery Company, or Case Company. The full shaving ritual consisted of the beard first softened with hot towels, prepared in a special steam cabinet. The razor would be honed on a leather strop, and kept sharp during the operation by means of further stropping. Lather was applied by means of a badger or hog's bristle brush, from soap mixed on the brush in a shaving mug. The blade was cleaned on wipes, which would have a dispenser and disposal bin. Other paraphernalia would include a sterilizer for combs and scissors, a neck-dusting brush and a hand-held mirror. Some shops had children's chairs; high chairs of porcelain enamel, and these are particularly sought after. All barbershop items are collectible, and razors themselves form a special theme for collectors who extend the period of interest to include safety razors, electric razors and ladies' razors.

Whereas barber's straight razors were strictly

ABOVE: *This impressive, large-scale molded plastic pegasus promoting Mobil dates from the 1940s. It is interesting to note that the symbols of major companies were so successful that the company name did not have to appear.*

functional, those produced for home use could be very ornate. Etched blades, ivory or pearl handles, and even gold or silver embellishments were not uncommon. By the turn of the century the safety razor pioneered by Gillette in 1895 had spawned a host of variations from such companies as Everready, the Gem Cutlery Company, Devine and Company, and countless others. Electric shavers hit the market in the 1930s, but it was not until the 1950s that a vast increase in electric shavers revolutionized men's toiletries. Much of the change can be credited to the success of the Schick Mode 20, designed by Carl Otto in 1950. The safety razor continued in use, however, rejuvenated by modern designs such as the American Safety Razor Company's 1951 Pal Stainless Steel Model designed by Henry Dreyfus.

The collector is spoiled by the range of domestic razors available, including early plastics, as well as by examples of the contemporary advertising, particularly those which appeared in popular magazines for Christmas and Father's Day. They provide often amusing images of the fashions of the times.

But the greatest example of vanishing America is in what used to be at the heart of daily life, the general store. It existed in two forms, the 'country'

Top: *Enamel and tin signs have an appeal to sign collectors as well as to gasoline and auto enthusiasts.*

ABOVE AND LEFT: *Blotters, such as these promoting tires and oil, were common forms of advertising.*

type, which still exists in touristically appealing versions in the New England and Midwestern states, and that victim of price inflation and changed shopping patterns, the 'five-and-dime'. From the latter, collectibles include fixtures like old cash registers, wooden counters and pigeonholes, and tin and enamel signs. The articles sold from these stores are in themselves collectible – Depression glass, china, toys and toiletries – and can be found elsewhere in the book.

RIGHT: *Automobile images are not restricted to motoring products, as exemplified by the stylish Art Deco graphics of this broom label.*

THE COUNTRY STORE

Although some genuine country stores still exist, they are an endangered species – so much that those items which can broadly be held to be evocative of such places are highly dsirable collectibles.

The country store was always more than *just* a shop, for it was also a social focal point of rural communities, a meeting place, post office and sometimes the only source of goods in a large area. The country store, like the 'five-and-dime', offers the collector a selection of store fittings and furnishings such as display cases, the shop bell, and string dispensers, for many goods would have been wrapped in parcels before the advent of pre-packaging.

BELOW: *X-ray vendor dispensed a gumball but also paid out tokens which could be redeemed for goods; 1940s.*

Goods sold loose meant weighing scales and weights, as well as a profusion of containers, bins and measuring scoops and tin containers used for products such as peanut butter, coffee, cocoa and tea. In smaller versions these tins were destined for the end user, but manufacturers also provided lavishly decorated large tins, jars and pails from which their product could be sold loose.

Sales would be rung up on the cash register, although a simple wooden single-drawer box with an integral receipt roll might be used instead. Cash registers began to make an appearance at the end of the last century, but among collectors the most highly regarded tend to be either the very small version which only rang up to a dollar – known as a 'Candy store register', since that was a common place to find these small purchase machines – or the magnificent brass and marble mammoths which graced the large emporiums. The register itself might be embellished with cast brass marquee, though it should be noted that many of these have now been reproduced. As each year brings us nearer to the 'cashless society', the clank and ring of the old cash register become more and more appealing. The marble or slate shelf – where the clerk could ring a coin if a counterfeit was suspected – the bell announcing a sale, and the cheerful 'call again' marquee, now bear silent testimony to a shopping experience which will never be repeated.

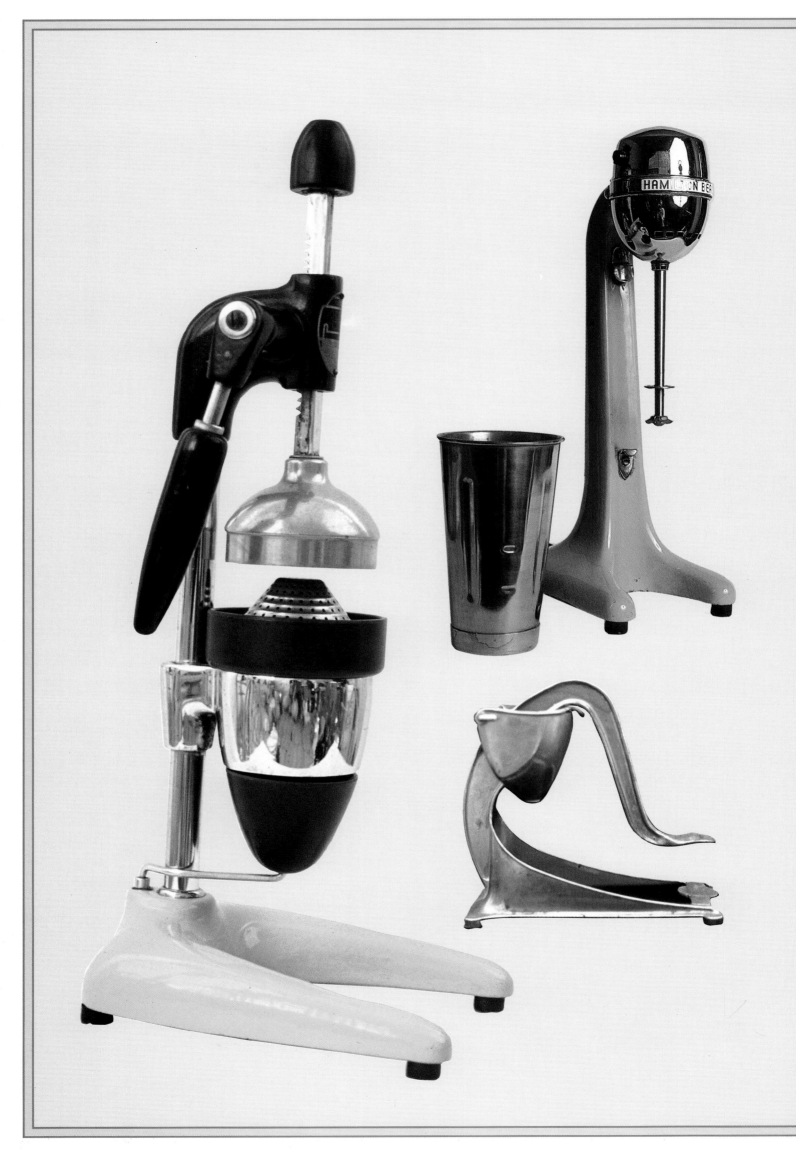

THIS PAGE AND FACING PAGE: A sample of store paraphernalia, including juice squeezers and milk shake makers, showing the range of designs that may be found.

TRAVEL AND TRANSPORT COLLECTIBLES

*S*ouvenirs from land, sea and sky that
evoke the romance of faraway places.

ABOVE: *The public have always
been fascinated by the
lifestyles of the famous. This
postcard shows the home of
Jane Withers.*

Exotic postmarks and scribbled greetings from far-away places are the realm of the postcard, now a highly collectible bit of ephemera. As a pictorial record of the changing faces of well-known landmarks and as a historical resume of the development of tourism, the postcard is both accurate and idiosyncratic. It appeals to collectors with both visual sense and a feel for popular history, and to amass a collection – whether of a particular place, of a particular era, or of a particular type of card – does not require a large disposable income.

Although postcards first originated in Europe in the 1860s, they almost immediately began to appear in America. Among early popular subjects were religious themes and reproductions of European works of art, while the American market was quick to enroll photography in its service, producing views of landscapes, townscapes and notable events. Because even quite parochial views became available as postcards, this makes them an invaluable source in historical research. Advertisers, too, quickly saw the potential of the postcard – particularly after 1898 – when commercially produced cards were allowed the reduced rate hitherto reserved for government-issued ones. Virtually everything and anything became a subject for greetings postcards, as well as for the souvenir type. The publication soon covered all the major events in the calendar, as well as Valentine's Day and birthdays. Other favorite subjects included children, animals, film stars and personalities, political slogans and war views, transport and humor. Among the novelty postcards were those with front flaps which open to reveal a concertina of folded images – usually souvenir views. Curiosities included linens, which were printed on a simulated fabric surface, and embossed cards. Postcard collecting became fashionable almost as quickly as sending the cards themselves, so that original early albums are sometimes available.

These albums are personally compiled versions of social history, and it is certainly preferable to see them left intact, even when only a small proportion of the contents are interesting cards in their own right. Some old postcards, particularly those of the 'naughty French' variety or which feature film stars, have been reproduced, so the buyer must take care to inspect cards carefully before buying. Usually the printing details make the newness of the card evident.

OCEAN TRAVEL

There are numerous chandler's fittings, nautical instruments and shipwright's tools from ships, among them Mississippi riverboats, whaling ships, pleasure and racing yachts, powerboats, steam

Never felt any better in my life

ABOVE: *Seaside 'linen' postcard, 1920s. Note the airship and airplanes of that era.*

launches and square riggers. The most popular of these seaworthy collectibles, however, are the fixtures and memorabilia of the great ocean-going liners which conjure up a magic air of romance and adventure from a vanished era.

The subject is dominated by the companies and ships which made the North Atlantic crossing between England and the United States, but other ocean routes are equally interesting. As well as the regularly scheduled routes, 'exotic cruises' were also popular. The Dollar Steamship Company, for instance, offered an 85 day round-the-world cruise for $750. The very names of the companies – Cunard, Olympic, White Star – and of the ships – the *Queen Elizabeth, Queen Mary, United States, Lusitania* and *Titanic* – summon up a whole lifestyle. Although the popular image was glamorous, it must be remembered that, hidden from the view of the beau monde travelling first class, were the poor migrants who crossed to America on the ships in stowage.

With their hundreds of crew members working behind the scenes, these ships were veritable floating cities. They were furnished with bakeries and kitchens, restaurants, cocktail lounges, ballrooms complete with the finest orchestras, jewelers, clothes shops, barbers, gymnasiums and steam rooms, cinemas, and even office facilities complete with stenographers. These services provide the collector with a wealth of products from which to choose. There would even be a print shop producing a daily newspaper featuring news gathered by the radio room as well as updates on the ship's own social calendar. The liners typified their period, with the gilding and opulence of the early 20th century superceded by the streamlined modernism of the late 1920s and the 1930s Art Deco. So synonymous were these ships with the new look that an early description of Art Deco was 'liner style'.

Ocean-liner collectibles encompass everything from postcards to matchbooks and ship's stationery, as well as everyday items like ashtrays, flatware from the dining rooms, lamps and other nicknacks. It was understood by the shipping companies that their passengers would generally pocket a few mementoes of the voyage. Ideal souvenirs then, collectibles now!

AIRPLANES

It was only during the last two to three decades that ships have lost their transatlantic trade to

LEFT AND FACING PAGE, BELOW LEFT: *Ships and boats exercise a fascination which has resulted in their being used as images on non-nautical items, such as these broom labels.*

airplanes. From the point of view of the collector of aeronautica, however, interest in postwar commercial flying, although growing, is far less than that in pioneer aviators, record breakers and military aircraft. Aviation came of age during World War I, and pilots who had learned to fly during the war began to offer commercial transport and limited passenger flights. The 1920s and 1930s were the romantic years of aviation, marked by such events as Charles Lindbergh's 1927 solo Atlantic flight in the single-engined custom-built Ryan, 'The Spirit of Saint Louis', which was followed the next year by Rear Admiral Richard E. Byrd making the first flight over the South Pole. In 1932 Amelia Earhart became the first woman to make a solo transatlantic flight.

Although by 1930 there were 43 airlines – including five international – operating in the United States, the poor economy had slowed the rate of progress in civil aviation. Crop-dusting pilots, unable to find work, became entertainers with their barnstorming aerial aerobatics in a Curtis 'Jenny' or Waco 9. These sky-high feats were popular during the Depression years, and like the feats of the more widely-known celebrities, brought glamor and excitement to dull lives. Memorabilia from these events are the object of much competitive collecting.

AIRSHIPS

On 6 May, 1937, having just completed its third transatlantic crossing, the airship Hindenberg exploded while docking at New Jersey. It spelled the end of an era. From the 1920s on, the airship represented the ultimate in travel. Bigger than most ocean liners (only a few feet shorter than the *Queen Mary)* the Hindenberg was luxuriously appointed, even possessing a ballroom. Because airships so captured the public imagination, they were frequently used as symbols of modernity, so that as well as items relating to the actual airships, the collector can encounter airship-inspired table-lamps and ornaments, as well as graphic items such as song sheets and fruit labels.

RIGHT AND FACING PAGE, TOP: *Menus from the great passenger liners are collected for their beautiful graphics and the bygone romance of ocean travel.*

BELOW RIGHT: *The variety of shipping lines and routes, some of which attract specialist enthusiasts, adds to the interest of the subject.*

CUNARD LINE

THIS PAGE AND FACING PAGE: *Miniature tin railroad signs were premiums for a breakfast cereal. Enthusiasts look back with nostalgia to the era of a multitude of railroads, each with its own personality.*

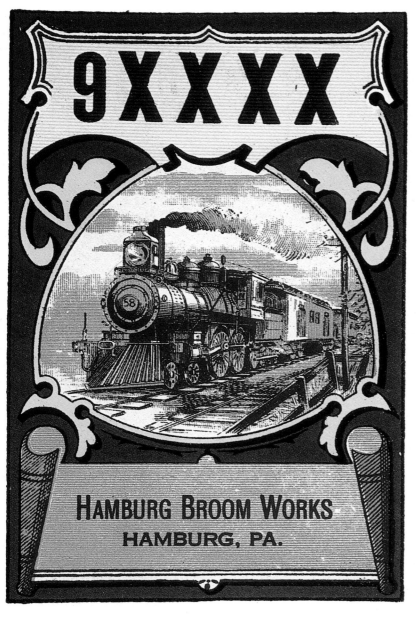

ABOVE: *The woodburning 'iron horse' locomotive is an evocative image of American history.*

RIGHT: *Breakfast cereal premiums – miniature tin railroad signs.*

TRAINS

From the woodburning 'iron horse' of the Old West to the streamlined splendor of the 'silver streak', trains have been an integral part of the nation's history. Particularly in the 1930s, when the future extensive use of airplanes was not yet foreseen, the railroads enjoyed an enthusiastic revival. The new locomotives and stock represented the highest achievements of industrial design, including the work of Norman Bel Geddes and Ramond Loewy. The Burlington Zephyr (known as the Silver Streak for its polished stainless-steel surface) was the star attraction of the 1934 Chicago World's Fair, while the other great trains – the Blue Comet, the Super Chief, the Twentieth Century Limited, the Broadway Limited, the Silver Meteor, the Electro-liner and the Sunset Limited – realized an idealized marriage of speed and luxury. In the early 1950s well-known figures such as Ronald Reagan extolled the virtues of train travel in advertisements, but by then its rivals – air travel and the automobile – were poised to take over.

So vast is the pageant of railroad history that many collectors choose one era, or one type of train, or one line in which to specialize. Train items include: advertising ephemera; timetables and tickets; dining-car china and flatware; conductor's and other employee's uniforms, hats and buttons; lamps, switch keys and tools.

HOTELS

The middle of the last century saw the advent of the great hotels, a natural corollary of both train and ocean travel. Romantic names like the Colony

License plates, traditionally produced in the workshops of state penitentiaries, were originally enameled on flat sheets, but in the early 1920s they became embossed metal. Although at one time they were valid for one year only, recently stickers have shown the expiry date. Various states – particularly those actively courting tourists – have incorporated an emblem or slogan to 'advertise' the state, and there have also been special plates, most particularly to commemorate the Bicentenary of Independence. License-plate holders have also been allowed to be used for advertising or a promotional purpose. Early plates seem to have survived in the more rural regions, hoarded as useful bits of metal for patching leaking roofs!

Hood ornaments range from the exotic crystal sculptures designed by the French firm Lalique, to the standard chrome versions riveted onto production cars. Motifs include birds, animals, nude ladies, Indian heads, planes and rockets. Some are endowed with a special feature, such as animation or illumination. Several hood ornaments have now been reproduced, and there is always the danger that these are being passed off as originals.

Hotel, Jerusalem; Raffles, Singapore; Shepherd's, Cairo; the Mount Nelson, Capetown; the Mamounia, Marrakesh – all became watering holes to the great and the literary. Hotel collectibles include luggage stickers, menus, postcards, ashtrays, china and flatware.

AUTOMOBILES

Although automobiles have long been a popular focus for the specialist collection, ranging from grand prix and classic sports cars to more prosaic vehicles, they do not fit within the scope of this book. However, the host of car-related material available does, whether it is collected to complement a car collection or as articles of interest in their own right. This area naturally coincides somewhat with gasoline collectibles, and includes sales brochures, postcards, sales premiums (model cars for children were often given when father purchased a new car) hubcaps, license plates and hood ornaments.

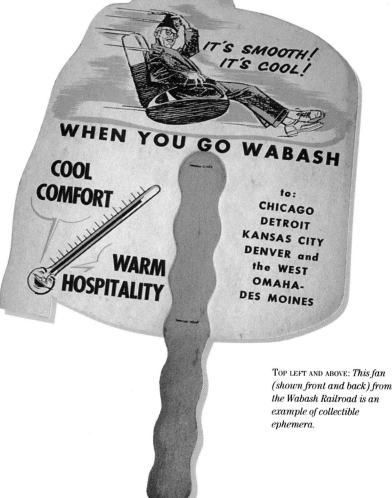

TOP LEFT AND ABOVE: *This fan (shown front and back) from the Wabash Railroad is an example of collectible ephemera.*

PENNSYLVANIA TURNPIKE TIRES

ABOVE: *Miniature tin railroad signs.*

ABOVE LEFT AND BELOW: *There is a contrast between the styles of these two metal signs: the traditional dating from the 1940s and the stylized 'turnpike' from the 1960s.*

PENNSYLVANIA
QUALITY TIRE SERVICE

EXP. 3-31-54

1953 PENNA

PT040

B260 GO-2
Contents—Merchandise.
Postmaster; This parcel may
be opened for postal inspection
if necessary.

General Mills, Inc.
623 MARQUETTE AVE. SO.
MINNEAPOLIS 2, MINN.

Return and Forwarding
postage guaranteed

NOTICE TO CUS-
TOMER: If it is
... to write this

Sec. 34.66 P. L. & R.
U.S. POSTAGE
PAID
MINNEAPOLIS, MINN.
PERMIT NO. 21

19 · VIRGINIA · 53

A59·30

MACK

PHOENIX
VALLEY OF THE SUN
ARIZONA

COMIC AND CALENDAR COLLECTIBLES

*R*eading for children and adults-only pin-ups – from strips to striptease.

ABOVE: *Comics have not always been for children only, as this first issue of* Sleazy Scandals *indicates.*

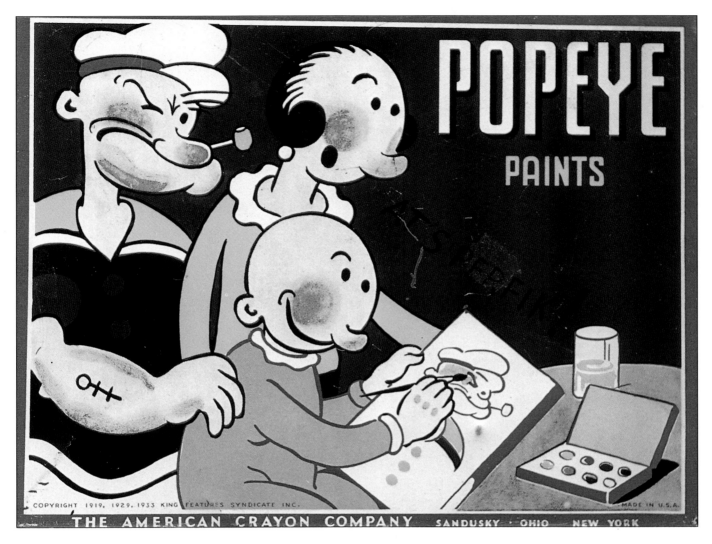

Above: Popeye and company were used to advertise such everyday products as crayons.

Cinema – and soon after, publishing – history was made when Walt Disney introduced the internationally-famous figure of Mickey Mouse to an eager public in 1928. He was followed by an army of much-loved characters. Astute licensing governed their transfer from celluloid to the printed page and countless products, assuring that none of the characters were debased. Other popular animated stars were similarly treated, including Orphan Annie, Betty Boop, Popeye, Bugs Bunny, Batman, Superman, through to Spiderman and beyond.

Although mass popularization owes much to this century's communication and entertainment media – the radio, cinema and television – the roots of cult cartoons can be seen in 19th-century newspaper comic strips, whose first starring character was the Yellow Kid. This impish street urchin appeared in 1896, and was one of the first comic characters to be represented in figurines and other novelties. Their age and scarcity put Yellow Kid items in the top bracket of cartoon collectibles, both in terms of price and status.

Another example of a graphic image going on to become a cult is of course Kewpie though she is best known as a doll. Serial comic strip adventures

were pioneered by Bud Fisher with his Mutt and Jeff, who began their daily newspaper appearances in 1907. Soon the 'funny papers' became a popular section of the newspaper. But by far the most successful of the early characters – who did not have benefit of the massive syndicating and marketing campaigns that more modern characters such as Snoopy or Garfield enjoy – was Little Orphan Annie. First appearing in 1924, the vacant-eyed waif built up a readership of some sixteen million. Annie's cheerful optimism symbolized for many the indomitable spirit of America's refusal to be beaten by the Depression, and probably accounts for her popularity during that time. Orphan Annie collectibles include figurines, dolls, games and puzzles, as well as the Big Little Books.

BIG LITTLE BOOKS

These books, which enjoyed great success during the Depression years, sold for only a dime. Although the name should properly only be applied to books by the Whitman Publishing Company who trademarked the title, other companies used the same format – about 5in high by 4in wide by 1.5in (12.7

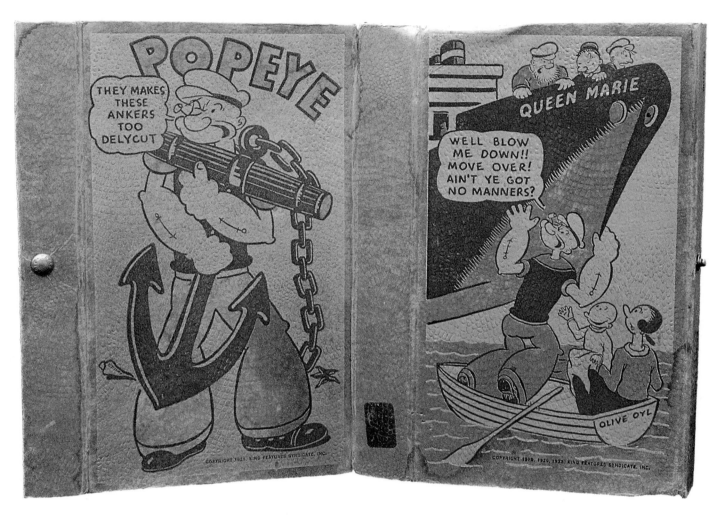

× 10.1 × 3.7 cm) thick, with bright cardboard covers and colorful illustrations.

Examples include Dell Publishing's *Fast Action* books, Fawatt Publishing's *Action* books and Soalfield Publishing's *Little Big* books. The Big Little books, as well as including sports titles and simplified versions of literary classics such as Tom Sawyer and Little Women among their number, mainly featured characters from the comic pages. In addition to Orphan Annie there was Alley Oop, Blondie, Dick Tracy, Lil 'Abner and Popeye. The cinema contributed such names as Jackie Cooper, Mickey Rooney and Judy Garland, as well as Mickey Mouse, Donald Duck, Bugs Bunny, Krazy Kat and Laurel and Hardy. Radio characters included the Lone Ranger, the Green Hornet and The Shadow. The high quality of the artwork of Big Little books has been a major factor in their recent popularity as collectibles. There is a high demand for examples in the rarely-found 'new' or 'mint' condition. Big Little book artists included Alex Raymond, Henry Vallely, Al Capp, Allen Dean and Will Gould.

The luxury version of the Big Little books were the die-cut pop-ups, introduced by Blue Ribbon Books in 1932. They featured much the same range of comic characters, and have experienced even a lower survival rate.

ABOVE: *The power of Popeye to sell becomes evident from the number of products he was used to endorse.*

FACING PAGE, TOP: *Calendar girl from the 1940s.*

FACING PAGE, BELOW Sleazy Scandals *issue no. 1, 1974.*

THE COMIC ALTERNATIVE

Although the Big Little books, under various guises by various publishers, continued into the television age, they eventually lost their popularity to the comic book. After their initial success in the newspapers, many of the early strips were subsequently reprinted, either as advertising premiums or for sale. The first comic book in the modern genre was 'Funnies on Parade', in 1933, while the first monthly comic was the ten-cent 'Famous Funnies' of July 1934. These were both shortly followed by King Comics Corporation, founded in 1936. In 1938 the most universal comic hero of all, Superman, was introduced in 'Action Comics', to be followed by a whole succession of super-heroes, including Captain Marvel, who entered the lists in 1940, Wonder Woman, Captain America, The Green Lantern, Hawk Man and Mary Marvel (Billy Batson's – aka Captain Marvel's – long-lost twin sister). The 1940s saw comic books reach enormous popularity, Captain Marvel alone selling at the rate of 2,000,000 copies every two weeks! During the 1950s, comics faced the twin threats of television competition and the hostility of parents and educationalists. The last were particularly concerned by the appearance in 1954 of a book condemning comics for,

CALENDAR ART AND PIN-UPS

As mentioned earlier, some collectors treat calendar art as a corollary to their own specialist interests, but these card-and-paper datekeepers are also collected for their own sake. Although the works of such artists as Maxfield Parish and Norman Rockwell have appeared on calendars, the term 'calendar art' is almost synonymous with the 'girlie' or 'pin-up' calendar. Whether these should be regarded as charming artefacts from the past, or as examples of degrading, exploitive sexism, will be up to the individual collector. But there is no escaping the fact that the pin-up – who became a popular image in the pages of *Esquire* magazine, on matchbooks, playing cards and the fuselages of World War II airplanes – also brought her artistic values to the walls of thousands of workplaces, and ended up by becoming a kind of American institution. The printing company Brown and Bigelow, the world's oldest and biggest calendar producers, issued the first girlie calendar 'Meditation', which featured an alluring young damsel, seemingly bare-breasted beneath her long, pre-Raphaelite tresses. In 1913 the first nude pin-up appeared, the notorious 'September Morn', which featured as a best-selling image on numerous other objects as well. Thousands of the calendars, including pirate productions, were sold.

among other things, causing juvenile delinquency. The author took special exception to the horror comic which had joined the ranks of super-heroes, detective, western and war subjects. The 1960s and 1970s witnessed a revival in comics, with a new generation of super-heroes accompanying renewed interest in the originals. It was also at about this time that comics began to be taken seriously, especially since pop artists like Roy Lichenstein and Andy Warhol contributed to this belated recognition in their own art. As a result several early super-hero comics were re-issued.

The ever-escalating value of comic collectibles has attracted much publicity, particularly from press and television. Their reports often pretend incredulity that a mass-produced ten-cent throwaway item from yesteryear can now be worth thousands. It is hard to understand why this attitude persists, as other cheap, mass-produced throwaways known as postage stamps have been taken seriously, considered valuable and collected for over 100 years! Whatever the arguments, comic books are now prime investment items, but the careful collector must know his subject. Condition is important – tears, spine damage, rusty staples, bent covers or foxing all affect the price. Keep valued copies in archival storage bags.

RIGHT *Playboy* magazine,
*Christmas issue December
1962.*

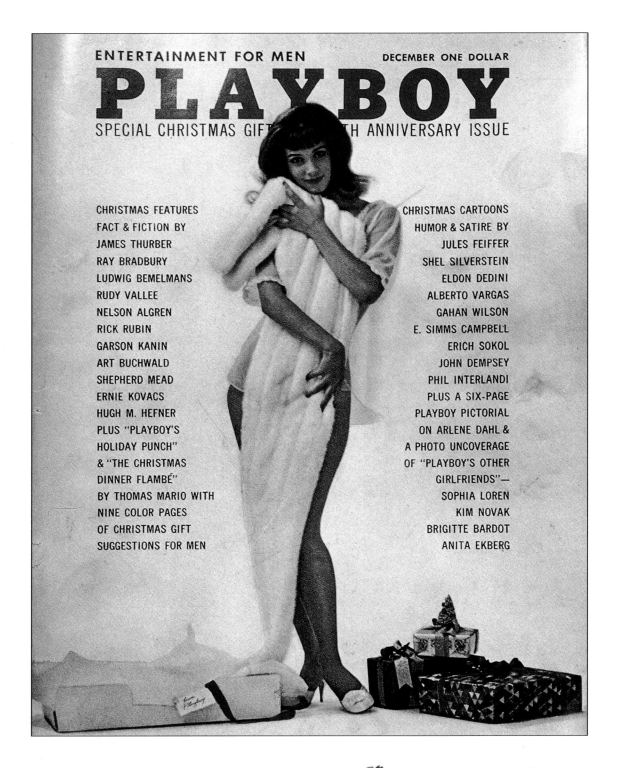

ENTERTAINMENT FOR MEN   DECEMBER ONE DOLLAR

PLAYBOY

SPECIAL CHRISTMAS GIFT   TH ANNIVERSARY ISSUE

CHRISTMAS FEATURES
FACT & FICTION BY
JAMES THURBER
RAY BRADBURY
LUDWIG BEMELMANS
RUDY VALLEE
NELSON ALGREN
RICK RUBIN
GARSON KANIN
ART BUCHWALD
SHEPHERD MEAD
ERNIE KOVACS
HUGH M. HEFNER
PLUS "PLAYBOY'S
HOLIDAY PUNCH"
& "THE CHRISTMAS
DINNER FLAMBÉ"
BY THOMAS MARIO WITH
NINE COLOR PAGES
OF CHRISTMAS GIFT
SUGGESTIONS FOR MEN

CHRISTMAS CARTOONS
HUMOR & SATIRE BY
JULES FEIFFER
SHEL SILVERSTEIN
ELDON DEDINI
ALBERTO VARGAS
GAHAN WILSON
E. SIMMS CAMPBELL
ERICH SOKOL
JOHN DEMPSEY
PHIL INTERLANDI
PLUS A SIX-PAGE
PLAYBOY PICTORIAL
ON ARLENE DAHL &
A PHOTO UNCOVERAGE
OF "PLAYBOY'S OTHER
GIRLFRIENDS"—
SOPHIA LOREN
KIM NOVAK
BRIGITTE BARDOT
ANITA EKBERG

BELOW: *'Girlie' waterside
decals, 1940s.*

From these origins grew the whole school of pin-up art, leading exponents of which were Rolf Armstrong, Earl Moran, Gil Elvgren, Fritz Willis, George Petty, Al Moore, and – generally regarded as the king of them all – 'Varga' Alberto Vargas. Varga's name is inseperably linked with *Esquire* magazine, whose pages had been originally enlivened by the eponymous 'Petty' girls. The 'Varga' girl first replaced George Petty's version in the calendar for the December, 1940, *Esquire*. Hitherto, girlie calendars had been used as an advertising medium. But with *Esquire*'s sale of 300,020 Varga calendars, the pin-up girl was launched .

The climate of World War II assisted the cult of the pin-up to flourish. While the fantasies decorated planes, lockers and walls, the real-life Betty Grable became an officially-endorsed morale booster for the troops. In recognition of such appreciation, *Esquire* patriotically provided some 6,000,000 copies of the magazine – specially printed for the troops and devoid of any advertising – free of charge during the war years, with a further 3,000,000 distributed to the workers on military installations!

Although the popularity of the airbrush-rendered pin-up continued, the postwar years saw the increased use of photography. The most famous photographic girlie calendar was the 1951 Marilyn Monroe example, published by John Baumgarth Company from Tom Kelley's 1949 photo session with the then unknown starlet.

LEFT: *General merchant's calendar for 1945 is typical of stock printers' calendars.*

CINEMA AND CARTOON COLLECTIBLES

*M*ickey Mouse rubs shoulders with
Marilyn Monroe in a roll-call of
memorabilia from the silver screen.

ABOVE AND FACING PAGE, TOP:
Snow White skittles game
exemplifies the countless toys,
games and other items that
owed their being to the
creativity of Walt Disney.

While comics were initially responsible for the creation of super-hero, the cinema was responsible for another aspect of American pop culture, the animated cartoon character. The first movie cartoon hero was Felix the Cat, introduced by Otto Messmer in a 1919 silent, 'Feline Follies'.

CARDBOARD MICE

Felix was a cult figure into the 1930s, and was used as a motif on a range of products, including nursery china, ashtrays and toys, as well as appearing as figurines and dolls. Although Felix was to enjoy a career as a newspaper comic strip from the 1930s to the 1950s, his cinematic star was outshone by the arrival of Disney's mouse.

The legendary Walt Disney has already produced a very successful cartoon character, 'Oswald the Lucky Rabbit'. Oswald, who actually looked a bit like Mickey Mouse, appeared in 26 Oswald silent films. Upon discovering that his contract with Universal Pictures had given them the rights to Oswald, Disney created a new character, first called Mortimer Mouse. Mrs Disney liked the character but not the name, and at her suggestion the mouse was called Mickey.

The first Mickey Mouse animated film was 'Plane Crazy' made in 1928 in the wake of the hysterical adulation of Charles Lindbergh. This was almost immediately followed by 'Gallopin' Gaucho'. But before either was released, Disney saw Al Jolson's The Jazz Singer (1927), the first talkie. Realizing that sound would transform the cinema, Disney made the third Mickey film, 'Steamboat Willie', into a talkie, with Walt himself providing the voice of Mickey. The immediate success of this, the first talking cartoon, led to 'Plane Crazy' and 'Gallopin' Gaucho' being issued with added sound. Within two years, Mickey Mouse cartoons were being made at the rate of about one a week!

MICKEY COLLECTIBLES

No fictional character has ever come close to the universal popularity of Mickey Mouse. Celebrating his 60th anniversary in 1989, the little rodent still entertains adults and children with undiminished success. His fans have included Franklin and Eleanor Roosevelt, Charles de Gaulle and Andy Warhol. No other character has been presented in so many different forms, making Mickey Mouse especially – and to a lesser degree all Disney creations – one of the biggest fields of collectibles. Why Mickey has such universal appeal defies simple analysis. But why so much collectible Mickey material exists is, however, simply because of the astute promotion Disney gave the character.

BELOW: *With so many thousands of Mickey Mouse items having been produced over the years it is not surprising that some collectors are happy to specialize in Mickey alone!*

The Mickey Mouse Clubs were founded in 1929, and cinema managers sponsored club events. Banks made Mickey savings banks to encourage young savers, while bakeries iced Mickey birthday cakes. Within three years the club had over 1,000,000 members in the United States, as well as clubs in other countries.

In 1928 Disney agreed to allow the use of Mickey on the cover of a school notebook. That deal made him $300, but he soon realized the even greater

PRINTED IN JAPAN

PRINTED IN JAPAN

RIGHT AND FACING PAGE, TOP:
Betty Boop and her friends captured the 'flapper' era in cartoon. These waterslide decals date from the 1930s.

FACING PAGE, BELOW: *Popeye has been one of those cartoon characters who have become embedded in popular culture. The doll's house chair is a good example of an ordinary item being enhanced through the use of a 'pop' image.*

PRINTED IN JAPAN

potential in marketing his characters. By 1935 Walt Disney Enterprises were advertising Mickey as the world's greatest salesman, with the capacity of generating $35,000,000 worth of sales a year!

The organized marketing of Disney creations began in 1930 when the George Borgfelat Company signed a contract to produce Mickey and Minnie Mouse handkerchiefs. This was quickly followed by dolls, games, toys, toothbrush holders and other items. In 1932 Disney, through Herman Kamen, began to license the production of items overseas. The control excercised by Disney over licensed products meant that although vast quantities of items were made, there was always strict fidelity in the representation of a character, the only variation being certified by Disney himself.

It also meant that the Disney image was never debased by characters appearing on inappropriate products. In 1933 came the most famous of all Disney items, the Mickey Mouse wristwatch. These were made by the Ingersoll-Waterbury Clock Company, from surplus US Army World War I watches, and retailed for $1.39.

The success was phenomenal, with Macy's selling 11,000 on the first day of issue alone. In the first two years, a total of 2,500,000 watches were sold. Production continued with new watches after the original Army surplus ones were exhausted, and in 1957 Walt Disney himself was the recipient of the 25 millionth Mickey Mouse watch. Even in the early days it was recognized that this watch represented something special. An example was sealed in the time capsule at the 1939 New York World's Fair.

Within a short time, the link between Mickey Mouse and the American Way of Life was acknowledged when Mickey became an official participant in the war effort. As well as being used on insignia and to decorate bombs and planes, Mickey appeared in propaganda films (alongside the educational and training films Disney also made for the government) and gave his name to the D-Day landing, the allies' password for which was 'Mickey Mouse'.

Although Mickey dominates the history of the Disney Studios and Disney collectibles, many other Disney characters are equally beloved. 'Snow White' (1938) made history as the first full-length animated cartoon film, costing a staggering $1,700,000 to make and grossing $8,000,000 in its first year. The 'Three Little Pigs' of 1932 became a symbol of the Depression era. Donald Duck and his family, Dumbo, Pinocchio, Bambi, all became incorporated into the nation's folklore, and the animation cels that went into making them come alive are now regarded as an art form. Animation – from the Disney and other studios – is unquestionably in the big league of collectibles, since the source of most original

TOP: *Pinback button featuring the little girl who captured the nation's hearts – Shirley Temple.*

CENTER: *Commemorative plate for the legendary James Dean.*

cels tends to be the major auction houses and specialist dealers.

DISNEY'S COMPETITORS

An artist regarded as Disney's equal was Max Fleischer, famous for the 'Out of the Inkwell' series of animated films and creator of the legendary Betty Boop. Betty typified the flapper of the Jazz Age, and was modeled on a real-life 'Boop a doop' girl, the singer Helen Kane. Her first appearance was as a nightclub singer in the 1930 Talkartoons film 'Dizzy Dishes'. She was later joined by her dog, Bimbo, and Koko the Clown. Fleischer pioneered the combining of real people with animation in 'Minnie the Moocher', when Betty Boop teamed up with Cab Calloway. Betty Boop collectibles include figurines, dolls, toys and jewelry, as well as the Betty Boop Radio and Big Little book stories.

Another Fleischer creation was Popeye the Sailor, who made his debut in a Betty Boop film. Popeye, Olive Oyl and Wimpey likewise inspired a range of products. The golden age of the cartoon, the 1930s also saw the birth of Warner Bros' 'Merrie Melodies' and 'Looney Tunes', starring Bugs Bunny, Elmer Fudd and Porky Pig. Although animated films, with the exception of The Disney Productions, eventually lost the massive audiences they had enjoyed in the 1930s, when audiences would sing along with Betty Boop as the bouncing ball made its way over the words, the tried-and-true characters continued to be featured in various products, so that many collectibles do not date from the original period. Television caused a revival in animated characters, for not only were old films shown but a new generation of television characters came into being. Of these the 'Flintstones' and 'Yogi Bear' can be seen as having the same sort of popularity as the cinema characters, with the inevitable rush of collectors.

FILM HEROES

At the same time cartoon characters were delighting audiences, live actors and actresses were also developing cult status. Movie collectibles encompass the entire history of the cinema, and while the greatest attention is given to original posters, lobby cards and pressbooks (publicity material issued by the studios), postcards and photographs – particularly those bearing genuine autographs – there is also the highly specialized area of artefacts from films or from the stars themselves. The most usual finds are costumes, but props, scenery and accessories are also included, and can be of very high value provided they have provenance – their authenticity and history beyond dispute.

programs were introduced to woo audiences back. Then the cinema became a mecca for escapism. Song-and-dance films were especially popular, but neither the sophistication and lavish sets of Busby Berkely, nor the skills of Fred Astaire and Ginger Rogers, captured the hearts of the nation as much as tap-dancing, singing child-star Shirley Temple. Her famous curls were inflicted on America's little girls while dolls, toys, games and figurines celebrated her cherubic charm. Franklin D. Roosevelt appreciated the enchantment of 'America's Little Sweetheart', commenting, 'During this Depression, when the spirit of the people is lower than at any other time, it is a splendid thing that for just 15 cents an American can go to a movie and look at the smiling face of a baby and forget his troubles'.

Shirley is still remembered for trilling the best-selling song 'On the Good Ship Lollipop'. Her films grossed over $5,000,000 a year, a huge sum in those days, and she was awarded a special Oscar 'for bringing more happiness to millions of grown-ups than any child of her years in the history of the world'!

Other cult movies of that period which are particularly rich sources of collectibles, include the Fay Wray *King Kong* of 1933, Bela Lugosi's *Dracula* (1931) and Boris Karloff's *Frankenstein* of the same year. The late 1930s and the 1940s saw Mickey Rooney and Judy Garland teaming up in a series of films, forerunners of the 1950s and 1960s teen movies.

The kings and queens of Hollywood required a court circular, to record the triumphs and disasters of the star system. The likes of *Silver Screen*, *Photoplay Screen Romances* and *Modern Screen* are now collected more for their lurid covers, sensational stories and pictures than for historical reference, since gossip and rumor were the main ingredients.

Some stars of the silent era, during which the Hollywood 'star' system was established, had their images used commercially in much the same way as the cartoon characters. Mary Pickford advertised cake mixes, while such diverse stars as Charlie Chaplin, Rin Tin Tin, Fatty Arbuckle and the Keystone Cops appeared on toys and figurines. But it was the death of Rudolph Valentino that put the seal on the era of star worship. Yet despite the presence of the likes of Greta Garbo, Douglas Fairbanks, and Jean Harlow, the star who was the biggest box office draw of the prewar era was a little girl – Shirley Temple. The Depression had initially seemed likely to kill off the movie industry, until 1931, when 25-cent double-feature

THIS PAGE AND FACING PAGE, BELOW: *The cult of Marilyn Monroe is demonstrated in her image adorning promotional items. (Right) a printed tin tip tray from the Playboy Club, mid 1950s; (opposite) a pocket knife from the same period and (above) a calendar for 1955.*

RADIO, RECORD AND TV COLLECTIBLES

*H*ousehold names from the magic boxes
and the items they turned into prime
investment material.

ABOVE AND FACING PAGE: The 'three little pigs' immortalized as figurines on a nursery plate.

Although the glamor of Hollywood endowed its stars with a particular charisma, the radio of the time was also creating household names. Radio had been popular since 1920, when mass production of sets began. But it was the simplicity of the mains plug-in of 1927 which brought an almost overnight national audience. Within a year production increased to about 75,000 radios a week, 85 per cent of the nation owning sets within a few years.

Very early radios and allied equipment, books and manuals, are highly valued and sought-after, but collectible radios tend to date from the 1920s to the 1940s. Recently there has been heightened interest in products of the 1950s and 1960s, particularly in early transistor sets. In the late 1920s radio was a status symbol, the big console models – particularly those which also housed a record player – representing the top of the market. Table models evolved from square boxes to the Gothic arch 'Cathedral' design.

In 1932 portable radios – which could be plugged into the mains or work on batteries – were introduced by the Emerson Radio Corporation. They soon led the market. Radio design echoes this liberation. The Sparks-Withington Company's 'Sparton' radios in particular chose the expressive lines and materials of Art Deco, including blue- or pink-mirrored glass, chrome and black lacquer. These were top luxury sets, but the newly-developed phenolic resin Catelin also allowed cheaper radios to be made in highly stylized cases.

Available in a wide range of colors, these early plastic models by Addison, Air-King, Crosley, Emerson, Fada, General Electric, Motorola, RCA and Zenith and others are among the most sought-after radios. The 1930s also saw a vogue for novelty sets, with the Majestic Company producing the molded metal Charlie McCarthy model and Emerson a range of pressed-wood Disney sets featuring Mickey Mouse, Snow White, and the Three Little Pigs.

These radios brought into the homes of the nation Roosevelt's 'fireside chats', the news of the Lundenburg kidnapping and the Hindenburg disaster, sport and the rising stars of the new medium. One show which lasted through the radio years was Amos 'n' Andy which ran continuously from 1928 to 1960. Two white actors, Freeman Gosden and Charles Correll, played Amos and Andy, as well as the other characters – Kingfish, Lightnin' and Henry – to a peak radio audience of over three million.

But the popularity of some radio stars in itself would not have produced the large number of personality collectibles which exist. This was due mainly to the commercial sponsorship of programs, so that manufacturers could make use of the character from their show for advertising material and other promotions. For example, the Wander Company made full use of their radio shows to promote Ovaltine, backed up by ingenious marketing. In The Little Orphan Annie Show of 1931, listeners were invited to send an Ovaltine label to the radio station, in exchange for an Orphan Annie Ovaltine mug and decal, while membership of the Orphan Annie Secret Society brought games, buttons and a special yearbook.

Annie was dropped in favor of 'Captain Midnight' in 1942, again with offers of special mugs and a support club. Midnight and his space crew transferred successfully to television, and the Ovaltine formula was repeated when 'Howdy Doody' became the Ovaltine TV character of the 1950s.

But the Depression years were the heyday of sponsored radio shows, with premiums proving irresistible to a nation which was counting every cent. Ralston, the cereal company, were early pioneers with a Tom Mix premium, and were responsible for the vogue for radio cowboys, like Gene Autry, Roy Rogers, Hopalong Cassidy and the Lone Ranger. These cowboy characters also later transferred to television. Until the cathode tube triumphed, however, imagination was fired by the purely aural adventures of Dick Tracy, who had his 'Secret Service Club', and official Dick Tracy wristwatches offered by Quaker Oats, while Post Toasties went one stage further with their 'Junior G Men' show, in which real-life gangbuster Melvin

ABOVE: *Moon Mullins and his associates: painted plaster figure made in Japan in the 1930s.*

LEFT: *Realistic bisque figurines of Amos 'n' Andy date from the 1940s.*

ABOVE LEFT: *Charlie McCarthy appeared on radio as a ventriloquist dummy who interviewed real-life celebrities. This tin toy by Louis Marx & Company dates from the late 1940s or early 1950s.*

ABOVE RIGHT: *Set of Orphan Annie figurines made of painted plaster, 1930s.*

LEFT: *This Orphan Annie watch, 'a guaranteed American watch for the American girl', dates from the 1930s.*

BELOW LEFT: *Emerson molded bakelite radio, 1930s.*

RIGHT: *Molded bakelite Pepsi-Cola radio, 1940s. This example lacks its original paper labels.*

RIGHT AND FACING PAGE, TOP: *The 'little luck god', Biliken, immortalized as a plate and a candy mold, made in the 1920s.*

Purvis, killer of John Dillinger, promoted Junior G Men kits. The ventriloquist's dummy, Charlie McCarthy, marketed as a 'personality', appeared as a figurine, a doll and even pioneered the chat show, acting as host to stars of the cinema and sport, whom he would 'interview'. Musicians, in particular, survived the Depression; though record sales had fallen, the 'crooner', (whose style was allegedly less likely to wear out radio tubes!) became the favorite sound of the airwaves. Kate Smith – the 'Voice of America' – achieved such popularity through her A & P Bandwagon that Franklin Roosevelt, on introducing her to the Queen of England, announced 'This *is* America'.

Bing Crosby, the Blossom Sisters, Paul Whitman and others boosted their sales of sheet music and records through the radio.

SINGERS AND CIGARETTES

The 1930s saw the public thirst for printed music reach new heights. Songs from films were particularly popular, though radio favorites ran a close second. While music from earlier times is also collected, examples from this period are especially regarded for the art deco graphics, often incorporating a picture of the singer who made the song famous. Sponsorship provided many bands with their own show case. Benny Goodman advertised Camels, while other cigarette companies also sponsored bands: Glenn Miller (Chesterfields), Tommy Dorsey (Raleigh), Artie Shaw (Old Gold) and Kay Kayser (Lucky Strike). Advertisements had the power to make cult heroes of their stock characters; Phillip Morris cigarettes used a real New York bell hop, Johnny Rosentinti, making him

a star in the late 1930s and early 1940s. Meanwhile, real stars were quick to realize the value of additional publicity, as well as of the extra income. Although early film stars had been tried in a few commercials, the 1930s to the 50s saw actors and actresses unabashedly endorsing name brands. Coca-Cola in the 1930s were the first to make extensive use of Hollywood stars like Jean Harlow, Greta Garbo, Johnny Weissmuller, Claudette Colbert, Cary Grant and Randolph Scott. By the late 1940s and early 1950s, all the popular magazines carried advertisements featuring various stars. One star in particular has been the subject of a recent collecting vogue – Ronald Reagan. He appeared in commercials for Chesterfield Cigarettes, rail travel and a hair preparation before becoming spokesman for General Electric, both in magazine ads and as introducer for their weekly 'Theater' program on television.

Although this sort of magazine advertising is now often removed from the magazine and offered as a 'tear sheet' collectible, the period flavor comes over better if the ad remains in its original context.

THE TELEVISION AGE

The growth of TV in the 1950s and 1960s saw a great influx of new heroes, as well as the revival of old ones. Among some of the most popular shows were old movies and cartoons, screened as cheap options. On 15 December, 1954, Walt Disney's 'Disneyland' television show commenced, its original purpose being the promotion of the Disney Park. The unexpected success of the Davy Crockett character, produced as a serial for this program, created the first TV-generated cult hero. The show

woodsman. It led to the current preoccupation with the market potential of children's television characters, now costed into the production budget.

Television show collectibles do not necessarily have to be old. In fact, many of the most popular 'cult' series like 'Star Trek,' 'The Munsters' and 'MASH,' are relatively recent. Nevertheless the survival rate of items like puzzles, toys, buttons, coloring sets and lunch boxes is notoriously low. Only a miniscule proportion will have remained in mint or even in very good condition. As well as concentrating on individual subjects, collectors of television memorabilia also follow themes – the great TV 'horse operas' or westerns, so popular during the late 1950s and 1960s. Notable among them were 'Cheyenne', 'Gunsmoke', 'Have Gun Will Travel', 'Wagon Train', 'Maverick', and 'Bonanza'. Detective series included 'Dragnet', 'Naked City' and 'Kojak'. Favorite comedies were 'Sergeant Bilko' with Phil Silvers, 'I Love Lucy' with Lucille Ball, 'The Show of Shows' with Sid Caesar. Children's shows, like the puppet programs 'Kukla', 'Fran and Ollie' (which enjoyed a peak audience of 10,000,000) and 'Howdy Doody' vied in popularity with family

attracted an audience of 40,000,000, and while the family cat went in fear of Junior turning it into a coonskin cap, a massive Davy Crockett industry came into being: caps, lunch boxes, toys and games filled the shops. Two hundred thousand surplus tents were hastily printed with the 'Davy Crockett' logo and sold out in two days. The record 'The Ballad of Davy Crockett' sold 4,000,000 copies within six months, by which time the craze had run full course. The legendary frontiersman had been worth an estimated 100 million dollars.

Though Davy Crockett items are not as highly regarded as those associated with the animated Disney characters, the statistics tell their own story, for how many of that $100,000,000 worth of goods have survived until today? Disney had not anticipated the overpowering success of the craze, and were slow to license official merchandise, so that many Davy Crockett articles were pirate productions. The popularity of the show did, however, create awareness of the massive potential for TV-inspired merchandise. Thereafter, nearly every small screen character was launched with the hope that it might prove to be another Tennessee

RIGHT: *'Superheroes' gained renewed popularity when television brought them to life from the comics in the 1960s. This record player dates from that time.*

RIGHT, BELOW RIGHT AND FACING
PAGE BELOW RIGHT: *Examples of
Hopalong Cassidy collectibles
include a cover, target game
and plate; all date from the
early 1950s.*

BELOW: *This nursery tin drum
dating from the early 1950s is
typical of the use to which
popular images were put.*

BOTTOM LEFT: *Roy Rogers
followed Hopalong Cassidy as
the cowboy hero, inspiring a
similar range of products.*

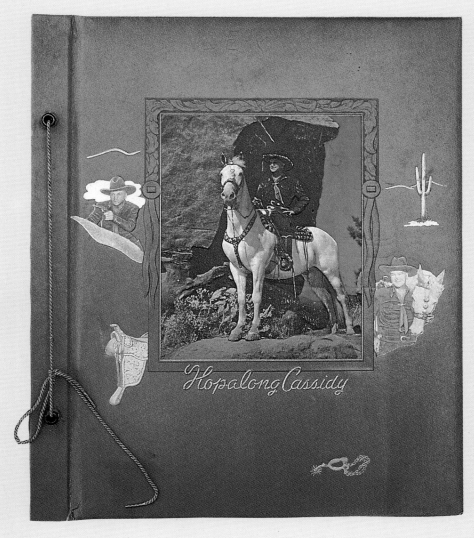

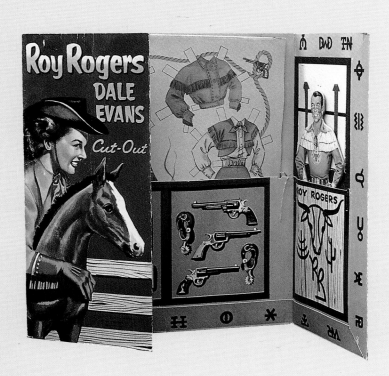

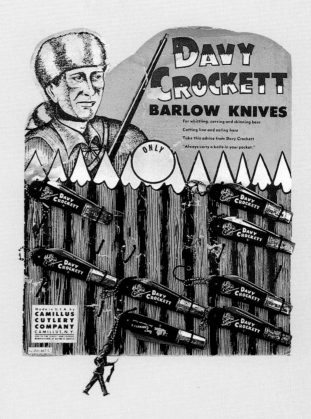

ABOVE LEFT: *The potential value of a popular image was enormous, as demonstrated by this Hopalong Cassidy publicity and exploitations 'manual', from the early 1950s.*

ABOVE RIGHT: *Davy Crockett launched the biggest bonanza of goods in the first major television-inspired craze.*

RIGHT: *Howdy Doody came to television in the New York area in 1947, and went on to become a nationwide children's favorite.*

ABOVE: *This cowboy gun, watch and badge set is an example of how a manufacturer would avoid a license fee but nevertheless capitalize on a character, in this case the Lone Ranger.*

shows like 'The Adventures of Ozzie and Harriet' and 'Leave It To Beaver'. Leading the market for children's promotional items was the school lunch box (see Chapter 13).

While the youngest market was realizing its full potential as consumers, another new market was developing, as teenage affluence coincided with the advent of rock 'n' roll. Donald Duck and Lassie were in the little league when compared to the exploitative 'pop singer' phenomenon. Rock 'n' roll memorabilia, once the domain of dewy-eyed adolescents, has now become the concern of the major international fine art salesrooms. Top items are

regarded as prime investment material. Although records themselves are collected, the bulk of rock 'n' roll collectibles is composed of contemporary and modern properties relating to major cult figures – Elvis Presley, Jerry Lee Lewis, Buddy Holly. Genuine autographed photographs, musical instruments, items of clothing, posters, and magazines, figurines, buttons and special-issue records represent the major part of such collectibles. However it should always be remembered that many items, such as Elvis' original Sun Label records, have been reproduced, and care must be taken when purchasing these artefacts.

LEFT: *The Lone Ranger, originally a radio character, went on to become an enduring television favorite. This game dates from the mid 1940s.*

NEWSPAPER COLLECTIBLES

A ll the news that's fit to buy (and some
that isn't!) – grist to the mill for real
enthusiasts.

ABOVE: Fortune *magazine for
December 1941 with a specially
commissioned cover by
Fernand Leger.*

Interest in social history is an obvious corollary to an interest in collecting. Even the least expensive and most ephemeral items can carry a strong 'feel' of an earlier time and place. Some of the most evocative sources of past times are old newspapers and magazines. Nearly everyone has discovered stored-away goods wrapped in an old newspaper, and found themselves smoothing out the creases to read it! American newspapers date to the beginning of the 18th century with *The Boston Newsletter*, but it was the 19th century, with its improvements in printing, in the fast communications brought about by the telegraph, and in the speed of distribution made possible by the train, that saw the introduction of the modern news journal. Collectors relate to their own local history.

A particularly popular aspect of newspaper collecting is a concentration of front page news –

ABOVE: *Mary Pickford graces the front cover of the* Illustrated Review, *1921.*

TOP LEFT: Illustrated Review *April 1921.*

ABOVE RIGHT: Pictorial Review, *December 1932, has a stylish front cover.*

RIGHT: Saturday Evening Post, *August 1938.*

major events as seen through the headlines. Though a collection of the front pages of *The New York Times, The Cleveland Plain Dealer,* or *The Boston Globe* would provide a march through the highlights of American history, the old adage that you can't believe everything you read in the papers is surely borne out by the rare issue (3 November 1948) of *The Chicago Tribune,* whose headline proclaims 'Dewey Defeats Truman!'

Unfortunately, magazines are still being despoiled by having advertisements cut out of them. Although these advertisements, particularly those by well-known illustrators or featuring film or radio stars, make great decorative items, they are still best appreciated in the context of the entire magazine in which they featured. At least since magazines have aroused increasing interest as collectibles, there is now a greater chance that they will be preserved intact.

The great age of magazine publishing was between the 1920s and the 1950s, a period distin-

LEFT: Colliers *magazine for September 1936.*

guished by an increase in cheap color printing and steadily increasing subscriptions. By the late 1950s high production costs and the overwhleming popularity of television were responsible for their decline.

Excluding front-cover art – a magazine collectible in its own right – the subject area can be subdivided into a variety of categories. Broad interest areas demarcated the buying public: family reading (*Colliers, The Saturday Evening Post, Life, Time, National Geographic*); women's interest and home matters (*Vanity Fair, Woman's Home Companion, Women's World, Good Housekeeping,* *House Beautiful,* and *House and Garden*); business (*Fortune*), as well as magazines for children, about hobbies or rural interests, and much more. Artwork by the likes of Norman Rockwell, Rose O'Neill, Maxfield Parish, or Varga, brightened the covers, while inside articles by important writers and studies by famous photographers, provide unique records of events sometimes unrecorded elsewhere. Magazines which are particularly collectible at the moment include those covering film, science fiction, fashion and sports. Many have a 'cult' following, especially *Playboy, Vogue, Mad* and *Modern Screen.*

GLASS AND CHINA
COLLECTIBLES

*Breakable and bankable goods that offer
the most varied choice of any collectible,
with something to suit all tastes and pockets.*

ABOVE: *A collection of carnival
glass, showing the vivid colors
that make it so sought after.*

and pottery was originally made in large quantities, the vicissitudes of time have ensured examples of sufficient rarity to stimulate interest.

The advent of press-molded glass in the 1840s allowed for more invention in design and greater economy compared to the previous technique of blowing. The glass used at this time was of lead-flint; the change-over in the post-Civil War period to lime glass, – a cheaper material – allowed for increased production. The burgeoning commercial market and growth in the numbers of salesmen and outlets in turn influenced the push towards large scale mass-production. Cheap colored glass was perfected in the 1870s, and by the 1890s there were over 400 factories producing large quantities of colored glassware. From this background and period come the bulk of glass collectibles. The two major areas for the enthusiast are those of Carnival and Depression glass.

LEFT: *Clear hobnail glass.*

Entire books have been written on the single subject of late 19th- and early 20th-century pottery and china – and, indeed, glass – so this chapter combining the two is meant as a brief overview, designed to give the interested novice an idea of the opportunities in both fields. The information relayed is concerned primarily with the material itself, rather than the forms which it takes, although there are many objects, such as bells, ashtrays, cups, inkwells and figurines, which command a large coterie of collectors no matter what their constituent material. For this reason, industrial and kitchen glass is excluded, with the exception of insulators.

INSULATORS

These sculpted knobs of heavy glass deserve a brief mention, if for no other reason than their unique fascination. They date back to the second quarter of the nineteenth century, and accompanied the introduction of the telegraph. The first patented insulator was registered in 1844, and was followed by a succession of designs brought out by a myriad of manufacturers and inventors. Over 500 separate designs have been recorded! Although prices and values are seldom mentioned in this book, it is interesting to note that the rarest insulators can now be worth in excess of two thousand dollars.

PRESS-MOLDED GLASS

Most popular collectible glass tends to be mass-produced. Though the majority of domestic glass

LEFT: *An unusually shaped blue glass vase with patterning.*

BELOW: *A hobnail milk glass vase.*

CARNIVAL AND DEPRESSION GLASS

As the name implies, Carnival glass was originally intended to be won as prizes at fairs. Although the type originally came from Czechoslovakia it was widely manufactured in the United States, and – as was much mass-produced American glass – successfully exported. It is characterized by an iridescent sheen, which is also to be found in the carnival-style post-Depression 'Iris' range by the Jeanette Glass Company. A unique type of carnival was Goofus glass, also known as Mexican Ware, Hooligan Glass, or Pickle Glass. Manufactured by several companies – including the Crescent Glass Company, Imperial Glass Corporation, and Northwood Glass Company – it is distinguished by the fact that its pressed designs are also painted. The impermanent nature of this paint explains its original decline in popularity, with the result that production came to a halt. Any surviving examples in good condition are much sought after.

The description 'Depression glass' is applied to a range of glassware dating from the early 1930s. Although it has sometimes been called Tank Glass, the more evocative name has become the one universally accepted. The Depression era officially began with the collapse of Wall Street's stock market on 24 October 1929 – 'Black Thursday' – and the economic effects continued to become increasingly severe until Roosevelt's New Deal of 1933 began the slow move toward recovery. The remainder of the decade was distinguished by assistance like the National Recovery Act, the Works Progress Administration, and the Federal Emergency Relief Administration. Finally, the demoralizing 'Brother can you spare a dime' image of the bleakest years gave way to a generally more optimistic mood.

Against this background, Depression glass became one of the few flourishing consumer items. Cheaply mass-produced, and in many ways a successor to the European-derived molded glass which had been given as fairground prizes, it boasted over 130 different patterns and styles. Each pattern encompassed an array of items, ranging from plates, shakers and bowls to candlesticks and vases. Nearly all these items are of a surprisingly high quality. The patterns are as varied as the uncompromisingly angular 'art deco' lines of the Indiana Glass Company's 'Tea Room' to the Venetian look of the Martinsville Glass Company's 'Radiance'.

BELOW AND FACING PAGE:
Samples of carnival glass.

If this was insufficient variety to stimulate the collector, there was also a staggering spectrum of color! In addition to uncolored glass, the most common hues were transluscent green, amber or pink, while rather less usual colors included a rich ruby red, azure blue, turquoise and black, as well as opaque variations, some with applied decoration.

From this it is obvious that there is no single Depression style. The only unifying factor is the era during which the items were produced and the market for which they were intended. It is indeed amazing that such munificence of design could flourish at a time when the specter of the bread-line haunted the land. To be constantly aware of

THIS PAGE AND FACING PAGE:
Pieces of carnival glass. It is virtually impossible to discover the maker of items or the date of manufacture, as carnival glass was rarely marked.

this background not only enhances one's appreciation of the glass but, more importantly, brings that added dimension of social history, essential to understanding the relative merits of various crafts.

Priced to be affordable when every penny was precious, Depression glass was sold for as little as three cents a piece through five-and-dime stores such as Woolworth's or Kress'. In 1936, a 22-piece pink 'Miss America' set by the Hocking Glass Company could be had from Montgomery Ward for $1.35, while a 44-piece luncheon set was only $2.98. Despite these low prices, the previously mentioned high quality – even luxury – of some pieces meant that they were regarded with great

pride. Other businesses were quick to spot the appeal of glass, and bought it in large quantities to give away as premiums. The luxury of a visit to the movie house was rationalized if a free piece of glass was included in the price of the ticket.

As an established collectible, Depression glass is subject to price fluctuations, particularly as research reveals new information on the relative rarity or desirability of various pieces. Furthermore, there is the hazard of reproduction pieces to contend with. The fascinating variety of designs ensures the wide appeal of the glass; but it also means this is very much a subject where some specialization is virtually essential. Only a book dedicated to the subject, of which there are several could hope to cover such an enormous field. Here are a few patterns and companies to highlight the variety.

NEW MARTINSVILLE GLASS COMPANY

One of the most popular patterns, 'Radiance' (1936–9), was so 'up-market' that some consider it not to be true Depression glass. Produced in red, blue or amber, it was sometimes heightened with gold or silver decoration. It is the opulence of the color rather than any great elegance of form that makes the pattern so distinctive. New Martinsville commenced production in 1901, initially making fairly plain opalware before moving on to pressed 'crystal'. Without the flashiness of 'Radiance', their 'Moondrops', introduced in 1932, possessed a more formal quality, particularly in the variety of pitchers offered.

JEANETTE GLASS COMPANY

'Cherry Blossom' (1930–9) is the quintessence of the Depression style, conventional in its delicate but unexceptional design. Jeanette were major producers of Depression glass, other designs including 'Adam', 'Cube', 'Doric', 'Poinsetta', 'Homespun', 'Iris', 'Windsor', 'Swirl', 'Sunflower' and 'Sierra'. Conversely, non-typical designs must include the strikingly art deco 'Tea Room' of 1926, as well as the equally deco 'Pyramid' of the same year by Indiana Glass Company.

Equally atypical are those ranges with fired on color, such as the Hocking Glass Company's 'Vitrock', or the china-like 'Chinix' by Corning Glass of New York. In fact there exist so many untypical styles as to demolish the myth of standard Depression glass.

Whereas Depression glass should surely be confined loosely to the era which gave it its name – despite an accepted tendency to extend it into the

'50s and even later – an age of some 50–60 years does not in itself guarantee that a piece of glass or china is collectible. However, at the other extreme, and at the risk of offending some people, modern 'collectors' editions', although assiduously marketed are outside the ambit of this book. Their manufacture and sales are artificially geared to a contrived collectors' market, thus removing the necessary sense of historical origin and unfairly 'improving' upon the accidental survival rate of breakable objects. Excluding limited editions, however, there are many areas where modern glass or china finds its place alongside earlier products. An obvious candidate for this is a company which has established such an important niche that nearly all its products are considered collectible. Fenton Glass is a case in point.

FENTON GLASS

Dating back to 1907, Fenton is mainly associated with Carnival glass and its natural successor, Depression glass. The latter period saw the introduction of the incredibly beautiful 'Lincoln Inn' range. Another popular design was 'Hobnail', in which the surface was dotted with a pattern of relief hemispheres.

So characteristic of the popular Fenton style are these 'Early American' dishes that at first it may appear to be the most manufactured pattern. This would be misleading, however, since Fenton, over the years, embraced thousands of different forms, styles and colors.

IMPERIAL AND DEGENHART GLASS

Just as the production of Fenton's 'Hobnail' formed a major thread in the history of American glass, so too, in a smaller way, did the 'Candlewick' pattern. Manufactured continuously by Imperial Glass between 1936 and 1982, there are over 650 sets and designs, the greatest range of which were produced in the immediate postwar period. Usually of molded crystal, colors varied from rich blues and reds to amber, black, pink and pale gold. Decoration included applied silver as well as engraving and hand-painted designs.

Another 'modern' glass, Degenhart, has as its main appeal unique graduations of color within a single piece. These subtle variations on a theme distinguished the range of pressed glass produced by the Degenhart Crystal Art Factory between 1878 and 1947. Many of the later designs were reproductions of earlier successful designs.

The Degenhart Factory also continued a family tradition of paperweight manufacture established at the beginning of this century. These paperweights are highly prized today.

OTHER GLASS COMPANIES

Continuing the litany of manufacturers who spanned the century, mention must be made of L. E. Smith Company, founded in 1907. The firm expanded from kitchen items into a range of colored glass during the Depression. The company still continues to manufacture reproduction and modern decorative glass.

Another company which could boast notable longevity was the Westmoreland Glass Company, founded in 1899. Closed in 1982, it was renowned for its milk glass, though it also produced at various times colored crystal, tableware and historical reproductions.

LEFT: *A carnival glass vase.*

PORCELAIN AND POTTERY

The same observations which opened this chapter are perhaps even more pertinent when applied to china. The golden age of dinnerware was the 1940s and early 1950s. As revealed in popular magazines of the time it was a period characterized by the gentrification of society, with elegant living a generally-accepted aspiration. This was supported by the relative affluence required to obtain it. After the fifties came a move towards informality. The accompanying increase in plastics saw a decline in large-scale dinnerware. Notable potteries included several from the Southern states. Among the popular wares they produced were the 'Blue Ridge' range and 'Coors Pottery', the 'Silhouette' range manufactured by Crooksville China Company and Gladding McBean and Company's 'Franciscan Ware'. Salem China and Stangl were two further forms. But in terms of sheer volume, the prize must go to the Harker Pottery, which at its peak could produce 25,000,000 dinnerware pieces per year. Although the company dates back to 1840, it is its products of the 1930s to the 1950s for which it is best known. Harker intensively marketed its 'Columbia Ware'. One Columbia pattern in particular, 'Autumn Leaf', still has an avid following.

ABOVE LEFT: *A ceramic plate featuring portraits of President and Mrs Eisenhower.*

ABOVE RIGHT: *Ceramic cowgirl and cowboy figurines dating from 1940s.*

DESIGNERWARE FOR THE MASSES

In the productive boom following World War II, Harker were known as progressives in modern industrial design, commissioning series by Russel Wright and George Bauer. Interest in 'designer china' – which had created a brief vogue for Coors' laboratory ware being adopted for domestic use – persisted for an unfortunately brief period. Notable contributions included the short-lived Museum Modern Ware of 1946, produced by the Castletown China Company with the assistance of the Museum of Modern Art. The designer of Museum Modern, Eva Zeisal, also designed 'Tomorrow's Classic' and 'Century' for Hall China and 'Town and Country' for Redwing. Stenbeaville Pottery commissioned Russel and Mary Wright to design their 'American Modern' range (1939–1959), now highly regarded in the current renaissance which has gripped industrial design. Its speckled glaze and rounded shapes made it a runaway best-seller.

Russel was also responsible for the 'Casual China' range for Iroquois China. This was considered too avant-garde for a utility china – the purpose for which it was intended – but became successful on the West Coast when it was re-named and marketed as 'California Modern'. Designer ceramics made their biggest impact on the commercial market, however, with Frederick Read's 'Fiesta' range for Homer Laughlin, first introduced in 1936.

'Fiesta' is most widely famed for its bold, bright colors and sleek modern lines, in accordance with the aim of Read to bring cheerful, informal and, above all, affordable modernity to the home. The buyer was given a choice of designs: a series of concentric bands, or a very pretty and delicate floral pattern. Although kitchenware *per se* is not covered in this book, it should be mentioned that in 1939 Homer Laughlin complemented the 'Fiesta range' with a bake-and-serve range, 'Fiesta Kitchen Kraft' – basic utility ware in 'Fiesta' colors. Recently a range of 'New Fiesta' has reached the retail stores.

Among other memorable mainstream contemporary designs were 'Harlequin', 'Carnival', 'Riviera', 'Rhythm', 'Tango', 'Jubilee' and 'Mexicana'. 'Harlequin' was a cheaper version of 'Fiesta', produced exclusively for F.W.Woolworth's. Also designed by Read, it was one of Woolworth's most popular lines, from its introduction in 1938 until the late 1950s. Production ceased in 1964. The extensive range of dinnerware and other items such as ashtrays and vases were joined by novelty animal ornaments.

'Riviera' dinnerware was an economy line introduced in 1938. Production was limited, and their rarity makes them prized collectibles. 'Carnival', dating from the 1940s, was given as a premium with Quaker Oats, for whom it was made exclusively. Another exclusively marketed line was 'Tango', sold through the McLellan Stores Company. Although similar to 'Fiesta' in color, the forms were rather more traditional. But bold colors were eschewed for 'Fiesta's' special issue, 'Jubilee', brought out in 1948 in four pastel shades to commemorate the Homer Laughlin's 75th anniversary. 'Rhythm', introduced in 1951, initiated a move away from deco-ish form by the use of subtle coloring.

FACING PAGE, ABOVE LEFT: Plate commemorating the Brooklyn Bridge, New York.

FACING PAGE, ABOVE RIGHT: Promoting the Great East River Suspension Bridge.

FACING PAGE, BELOW: A souvenir plate featuring the Statue of Liberty.

BELOW: Carnival glass vase.

SOUTH OF THE BORDER CERAMICS

An individualistic variation of 'Fiesta' was the 'Mexicana' range of 1938. This appeared during a time when an interest in the 'Latin' look, already reflected in the bold primaries in Read's other pottery, reached its peak. Mexican theme decoration was also manifest in lines made by Paden City, Vernon Kilns (whose products also included a range of Walt Disney figurines, as well as decorative china) Crown and Stetson. In addition to 'Mexicana', Homer Laughlin also had a line called 'Arizona', which was produced only in small quantities and is therefore especially valued. 'Conchita' and 'Hacienda', also captured the South-of-the-Border flavor. All of these ranges had applied pictorial decoration with cacti, marachis and sombreros emphasizing the theme.

MASS CONSUMPTION

Although emphasis has been given to the 'Fiesta' and allied styles, Homer Laughlin, produced an enormous range of tablewares. Its history, from its foundation as Laughlin Brothers in 1871 to its modern capacity of over 45 million pieces a year, can be seen as another example of a company spanning the history of mass production. Some of these, as previously mentioned, were manufactured exclusively for large retail firms to market. A particularly successful example of this from the Homer Laughlin stable was the 'Americana' range, produced between the mid–1940s and mid–1950s, exclusively for Montgomery Ward. Pictorially decorated in the 19th-century English Staffordshire style, but with illustrations of American life and traditional scenes reminiscent of Currier and Ives, this – and the parallel 'Historical American Subjects' range – were found in homes across the East Coast and Midwest. A rarer collectible is their 'Nursery' line, much sought after by the top rank of dealers and collectors.

The output of many smaller producers must be viewed alongside those of the major manufacturers to complete the picture. But, this is not an attempt at a comprehensive listing, and excludes 'fine art' ceramics.

Highly regarded for its superb quality, the Frankoma Pottery produced dinnerware, jewelry, novelty items, and a series of special plates and limited-edition vases. Gonder Pottery which flourished between 1941 and 1957 was mainly known for its beautiful glazes. Its master potters also produced a range of reproduction antique crackle-glaze pieces.

The Hull Pottery began in 1917 as the A. E. Pottery Company, manufacturers of art pottery. The

THIS PAGE: *pieces from the
'Fiesta' range made by
Frederick Read for Homer
Laughlin.*

firm later expanded into novelties and kitchen-ware, changing to the name by which it is now known in 1950. Other manufacturers of art pottery included Morton Potteries – under which title is included the Cliftwood Art Potteries. These three together are inextricably intertwined with Morton history. Niloak Pottery was revamped and renamed the Eagle Pottery in 1929. It is especially known for its Mission Ware, as well as for novelty and giftware items.

The Haviland Company was founded in France in 1842, but did not open an American division until 1936, when a native American decided that the time was ripe to introduce his fellow country-men to American porcelain crafted on the Euro-pean tradition. Since that time its development in the United States has reflected the trends affecting the entire craft. Further endorsement comes from the fact that Haviland dinnerware is a traditional favorite of presidents for use in the White House! But a word of warning to those with the ambition to assemble a comprehensive collection – there are over 66,000 patterns including variations! An-other big volume producer of dinnerware was the Shawnee Pottery Company, who also made art pot-tery. Founded in 1932, it could produce up to 100,000

ABOVE: *The base of a 'Fiesta' piece; the range was first introduced in 1936.*

TOP: *A coffee set in immaculate condition.*

BELOW: *A yellow glazed ashtray.*

pieces a day. Among its designs in which new inter-est is being shown are 'Cameo', 'Cheria' and 'Diova'.

China and glass must offer the most varied choice of any collectible. In terms of patterns, colors and period there is something to suit all tastes and pockets. Collectors' interest has, how-ever, created a wave of reproductions – some more or less 'authentic', as they are made from original molds or by the original factory – others spurious. These latter often fail to capture the original colors, and tend to lack the definition in relief-work possessed by the authentic pieces.

Of paramount importance is the condition of a piece; mint or fine is almost mandatory. When you read of items produced in their thousands the high incidence of casualties broken during manu-facture becomes easily appreciated. Added to these are all the items discarded after years of service. Nevertheless, miraculously, there are usually suffi-cient quantities of all but the most valuable varie-ties to make the acquisition of choice examples possible. Also remember that when a piece has survived against all odds, it is your duty to keep it that way. Some modern detergents can cause damage, so if you have any doubts about cleaning an item, leave it until you've consulted an expert!

CHILDREN'S COLLECTIBLES

The large world of little people encompasses ultra-sophisticated Barbie dolls, simple stuffed toys and hand-made marbles.

ABOVE: *Swirls such as these are only part of the world of marbles, and even these represent only a sample of the variations available. Obviously there is no chance of the marble collector becoming bored!*

DOLLS

Dolls have been with us since ancient times. Traditional materials include straw, clay, wood, rag and, in recent centuries, bisque porcelain; while innovations in the last 60 years include rubber, latex, plastic and vinyl. The variety of dolls has increased with an incredible momentum during this century as a result of technology and mass production. A brief chronological survey of these innovations shows the development of the 'modern' doll, though each year manufacturers vie with one another for even greater novelty. Recent phenomena include the personalized Cabbage Patch doll, complete with birth certificate, as well as a doll that can carry on a conversation. Despite such sophisticates – which are earmarked today as tomorrow's collectibles – it is the inherent character of each doll that provides its appeal.

BELOW: *A Rose O'Neill 'kewpie' doll – still produced today, though now as a limited edition.*

A DOLL CHRONOLOGY

1915: 'Sleep eyes' introduced by the Ideal Toy Corporation of Brooklyn, New York (founded 1903).
1930s: EFFanBEE Dolls (part of Fleischaber & Baum) pioneered the use of rubber. They also brought out Patsy, the first doll to be offered with her own wardrobe of outfits.
1939: Ideal Toy Corporation – the first company to exploit the properties of plastic for doll manufacture – introduce 'magic skin' finish.
1946: Horsman Doll Company bring out 'fairy skin', followed by
1952: 'miracle hair' and
1954: 'super flex'.
1959: Mattel Inc. introduced Barbie.

America did not have a tradition of bisque-headed dolls, although they were imported in large quantities in the 19th century, mainly from France. Dolls made prior to the 20th century, whether imports or home products, generally can be seen as more on the level of 'serious' antiques rather than as collectibles.

One doll, whose traditional style spans from the last century into this, is the Bup. The children of the Amish religious sect were allowed dolls, as long as they were faceless. This precept was observed in order not to transgress the biblical command forbidding graven images. Often made by the children themselves, these dolls are valued as examples of folk art, possessing an innocent charm which the commercial products lack.

DOLLS AND CLOTHES

No greater contrast could there be to the simplicity of the Bup than the ultra-sophisticated Barbie doll. Although the German Lilli doll is sometimes credited with being her forerunner, Mattel Inc. (which had bought the rights to Lilli) caused a sensation in the industry with this famous teenage fashion doll. The most controversial aspect was that Barbie had a figure – as the weekly New York newspaper the *Village Voice* put it, 'boobs in Toyland', Barbie not only acquired a doll boyfriend, Ken, as well as sister, dog and friends, but also thousands of costumes and accessories. Because of this she can be seen as a detailed and accurate record of American fashion and lifestyle trends over the last 30 years. To many, the fascination of Barbie makes her more of a cult figure than a collectible. Since her birth in 1959 Barbie has undergone subtle changes, and Mattel's policy of allowing a trade-in of old Barbies when new models were introduced has made the early ones especially sought after.

THIS PAGE AND FACING PAGE: *A sample of the variety of forms taken by dolls: commercial and handmade, black and white, cloth and plastic.*

Although no other doll has come close to Barbie in terms of doll 'lifestyle', other companies have nevertheless produced dolls whose wardrobes, as much as the dolls themselves, are the prime selling point. Vogue Dolls, which began as a manufacturer of doll clothing, introduced its own doll during World War II. The Ginny doll, a favorite in the late 1940s and 1950s, boasted over 100 different costumes.

Costume dolls – those which wear period or national dress – are a collectible in their own right. These are not 'dressing up' dolls, and their costumes are generally of a very high quality.

Highly-prized examples of the costume doll are still made by the Madame Alexander Doll Company of New York which commenced production in 1923. In addition to the 1960s 'international' series of national costumes, Alexander produced the Dionne Quintuplet dolls in the late 1930s, and other 'portrait' dolls, including Scarlet O'Hara and Prince Charles. Other of their favorite character dolls included the Louisa May Alcott's four 'Little Women', Cinderella and Snow White. Mollye Dolls produced miniature ideals of Martha Washington, Judy Garland, Ginger Rogers, Princess Elizabeth and even Mamie Eisenhower! Another manufacturer of 'portrait' dolls was the Ideal Toy Corporation, which 'cloned' Shirley Temple, Judy Garland and Deanne Durbin, as well as introducing a black doll, Sarah Lee. Black dolls are much sought-after, particularly early examples with realistic black features rather than white dolls painted black. These 'realistic' examples usually come from France or Germany, although since the 1950s several American companies have made black dolls. As well as Sarah Lee, there were Miss Black America and a black baby doll, both by EFFanBEE. Mattel's Barbie was joined by Black Frankie, followed by Black Christie at the end of the 1960s.

CHARACTER DOLLS

Character dolls are those whose design – particularly facial features – endow them with a distinctive 'personality'. Many of these were made by the American Character Doll Company founded in 1918. Recent characters include Holly Hobbie (from the Knickerbocker Toy Company) and Raggedy Ann and Andy (by Mollye Dolls). The all-time classic character – still in production although as a limited edition today – is the Rose O'Neill 'Kewpie' doll. Making its first appearance as an illustration in 1909, Kewpie, whose whimsical, mischievously expressive face combines the human infant and a fairy like character had an obvious appeal. Kewpie first appeared as a doll in 1913, and has been produced in various forms – including

pirate copies – ever since. Kewpie is collectible in her own right, for in addition to dolls there are many different items decorated with the Kewpie design.

FOREIGN SUPPLIERS

As massive consumers of toys the United States has attracted many imports. Except in the cases of certain large and historic companies such as Stieff and Britain's, they have not been included in this summary. Thus most space toys and robots are excluded, since they are nearly always Japanese, as well as the majority of prewar toy soldiers from Britain and France, as well as die-casts by Dinky and Matchbox from Britain. There are more than sufficient suppliers to keep the patriotic collector happy in the following categories.

STUFFED TOYS

Although many American companies have produced stuffed toys, the commercial leaders in this field, also credited with being the pioneers of mass-produced soft toys, is the Stieff Company of Germany, much of whose production has been exported to the United States. Stieff stuffed animals are very collectible, and prices for both new and old models are high.

It should be mentioned that although Stieff 'invented' the teddy bear, it was the Ideal Toy Corporation that was the first American teddy manufacturer, and of course it was an American, president Theodore Roosevelt, whose name was bestowed on this much-loved toy. Ideal still ranks as one of the major producers of stuffed toys in the United States.

PAPER DOLLS

These have their origin in 19th-century Europe, where quite elaborate kits, including theaters with their own cast of players, were very popular. In the United States magazines included cut-out paper dolls as a novelty promotion.

In the 1920s cut-out paper doll books were introduced. They proliferated through the Depression years, helping to alleviate the toy shortage during World War II (when industries moved into war production and restrictions on the usage of metal and plastic also helped bring about a revival of wood and rag toys).

The 1940s and 1950s saw the introduction of 'celebrity' paper dolls, including Grace Kelly and Marilyn Monroe. Such paper dolls are produced to this day, although the end of the 1950s marked their decline.

TOY SOLDIERS

Sometimes called 'dime-store soldiers', because they were sold by 'five-and-dime' retail outlets, these cheap toy soldiers were immensely popular from the mid-1930s until World War II put an end to virtually all toy production. As most of these soldiers were made of cast lead (some, however, were of iron and plastic), it was the war that not only curtailed their production but also caused many to be destroyed in scrap drives. As a result, despite the thousands made, they are now relatively rare.

The main producers of toy soldiers were the Barclay Manufacturing Company of Hoboken, New Jersey (1913–71), and Manoil Manufacturing Company of New York, who flourished from 1937–41. Among the smaller American producers are Auburn of Auburn, Indiana (flourished 1913–68), while the world's largest was William Britain of London (founded 1893), whose soldiers were much collected in the US. Civilian versions of the dime-store soldiers included cowboys, indians, and policemen, although it was the soldiers, particularly in view of the strong militaristic mood prevailing immediately prior to the war, that had the greatest popularity.

METAL TOYS

The first American cast-iron toys appeared in the late 1850s and early 1860s, and by the 1880s and 1890s, the craft was in its golden age. The classicists among collectors often set their cut-off point at the turn of the century, but for collectibles the net extends wider and later. The following are among the makers worth special consideration.

The Arcade Manufacturing Company was founded by the two Morgan brothers in Freeport, Illinois, in 1868, and by the end of the 19th century had diversified from its original light industrial production into coffee mills and toys. Its first hugely successful toy, however, did not appear until the 1920s – it was a model of the popular yellow cab that plied the streets of New York and other major US cities. From that, the company expanded into toy banks, cars, doll furniture and character toys like Andy Gump. At the outbreak of World War II, it still had over 300 toys on its active work books. But the war spelled its doom and the company closed down in 1946.

Arcade's advertising slogan was 'They Look Real', while that of Hubley Manufacturing Company (founded 1894) was 'They're Different!'. Though both companies were competitors, Hubley avoided the slump that affected other rivals during the Depression by changing to cheap penny toys. While

ABOVE: *Paddle-type tin clacker, made by T. Conn, probably 1950s.*

BELOW: *The passengers give additional charm to this tin San Francisco cable car; dates from the 1930s.*

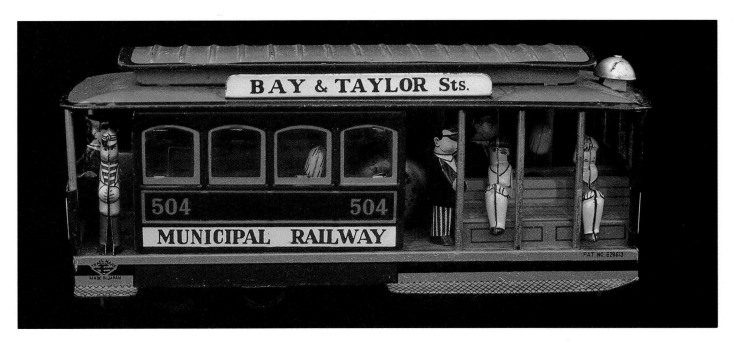

TOP: *Cast-iron brewery wagon by the Hubley Manufacturing Co., c 1920s.*

CENTER: *Although as much souvenir items as pure toys, the San Francisco cable car has always been a popular subject. This tin example dates from the 1950s.*

BELOW: *Example of a magnificent old-style fire truck in metal dating from the 1930s.*

TOP: *Although not a toy, this metal funeral car, made as a modern limited edition, is in keeping with the tradition of American cast metal collectibles.*

CENTRE: *A 1930s fire truck made of metal.*

BELOW: *Ives, makers of this model 3251 locomotive, were, alongside American Flyer and Lionel, the leading makers of toy trains.*

TOP: *A 'Department of Sanitation' truck seems an unlikely subject for a toy. This realistic tin example dates from the early 1950s.*

CENTER: *Tin sedan car, early 1950s.*

BELOW: *Articulated tin rescue truck, 1950s.*

TOP: *'Buddy L' Toy Company was famous for large-scale metal toys, such as this pick-up truck from the 1960s.*

CENTER: *This tin ambulance has opening rear doors and comes complete with a stretcher; 1940s.*

BELOW: *Large-scale Greyhound bus, early 1950s.*

cast-iron fire-engines, circus wagons, trains and farm wagons were their original staples, model cars became the top sellers in the 1930s. Wartime iron quotas spelt the end of the toy division in 1942, though the company continues as a division of CBS.

Even without the Depression and war, the lifetime of the clumsy cast-iron toy was over by the mid 1930s. The development of precision die-casting allowed lighter-gauge metals to be used, giving finer detail. Cast-iron toys, nevertheless, have a primitive charm, and their material often makes them seem older than they are. Many of the companies which produced cast-iron toys also worked in die-cast metal and lithographed tin, a popular process imported from Germany. Plastic too began to intrude on the market in the 1930s, especially when lightness, detail and cheapness were of prime concern.

Among the later companies to enter into the fray was the 'Buddy L' Toy Company of Salem, Massachusetts, whose initial lines of pressed steel pick-up trucks, issued in 1921, grew into a veritable army of cranes, steam rollers, and Caterpillars, grinding their way along floors and rugs even today. Many of their vehicles are on an impressively large scale.

Louis Marx & Company was one of the four major makers of electric trains during the Depression, as well as being notable for its large production of lithographed tin wind-up toys from 1919 on. Acquired by Quaker Oats in 1972 and then by a European firm, the Marx division declared

ABOVE: *Unmarked clackers, likely to have been manufactured by T. Conn, 1950s.*

FACING PAGE: *'BO plenty and sparkle' is a tin wind-up by Louis Marx, 1938.*

BELOW: *The 'Bing Crosby' junior jukebox made of metal and plastic was a nursery record player that actually worked; early 1950s.*

bankruptcy in 1979. The fabulous auction of its collection of stock from 1920 to its closure gathered collectors from around the world.

A company that has fared better in its fortunes is Fisher Price Toys, of Aurora, New York. Founded in 1930, it too was acquired by Quaker Oats, but flourishes in profits and reputation. The company was both an early user of plastics and early producer of learning toys, while scores of Disney characters were featured in its catalogs from the 1930s and 1940s. Any item made all or partly of plastic dates from after 1949.

Two more companies whose major production carried on between 1920 and the late 1940s should also be mentioned. They were the Kenton Hardware Company of Kenton, Ohio, and the Kilgore Manufacturing Company of Westerville, Ohio. Both specialized in high-quality cast-iron toys – trucks, fire-engines and cars – in the case of Kenton, to include toy stoves and banks, and in the case of Kilgore, cap guns and caps.

Finally, even the briefest survey of small collectibles must mention Crackerjack toys, those first collectibles of so many childhoods. The initial suppliers were a firm called Tootsietoy, who began making small novelties in 1911, although only after 1930 is the name shown on the toys. Crackerjack surprises from all the supplying companies are now much collected, though Tootsietoys remain among the best quality. In pre-World War II years, the company produced realistic small models of automobiles and airplanes; these experienced a fall in quality during the years during and immediately after the war. But by the late 1940s, the diecasts were again at a high standard.

TOP LEFT AND RIGHT: *Korean War period tin military vehicles.*

BELOW: *Tin US army truck by Louis Marx and Company, 1950s.*

PLASTICVILLE

While plastic has been given a passing mention in this chapter, it has been ignored as a subject in its own right. To continue this omission would be to ignore Plasticville, a collectible that authentically records the architecture of the American townscape. These snap-together molded plastic kits were primarily designated to go with toy trains. Their manufacturer, Bachmann Brothers Inc., had moved into plastics after a varied history that had begun in the last century as ivory workers. After a modest start in 1949, production of Plasticville blossomed into a range of realistic model diners, filling stations, and houses in varying styles – in short, everything needed to create a miniature town. The little buildings were produced in a varity of scales to suit the choice of model trains. I favor the term 'model' rather than 'toy' as a tribute to the high quality of detail achieved by such manufacturers as Ives, American Flyer and Lionel.

ABOVE: *Plasticville, a relative newcomer to the world of toy collectibles, preserves in miniature the American townscape of the 1950s.*

LEFT: *Molded plastic gasoline truck, late 1940s.*

ABOVE AND BELOW: *Plasticville miniatures of 1950s America.*

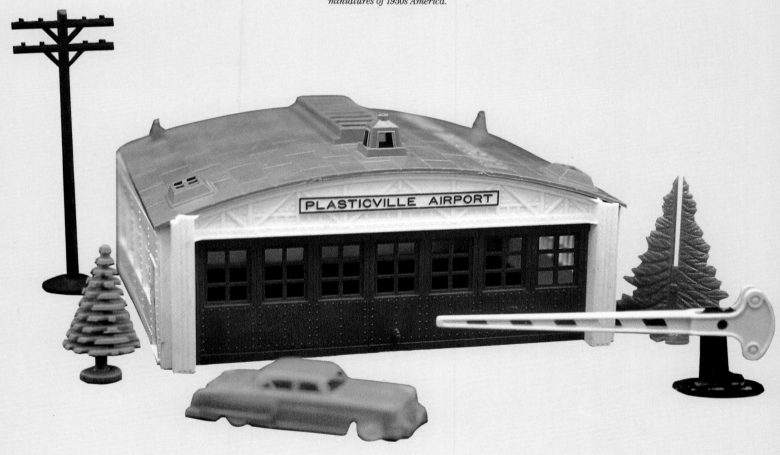

TRAINS

Trains have possessed a special romance, even when toy-sized. The train had played such a major role in the opening up of the country during the 19th century and its transport supremacy was only eroded after World War II by air and space travel, that it was a natural candidate for male pre-occupation. It has long been an accepted tradition of family life that Dad buys a train set as much for his own enjoyment as for Junior's. Although low-budget trains continued to be made as tin wind-ups, during the 1920s through to the late 1950s, the best examples were electric powered. The three factories of the Lionel Corporation of New Jersey produced over three-quarters of the nation's loco-motives and cars and accessories. Although more recent train sets have their enthusiasts, the extensive use of plastics today is generally regarded as a blow to quality.

ABOVE: *An Ives gauge o electric locomotive shown with Ives and Lionel carriages, c 1932.*

LEFT: *Two gauge o electric locomotives made by Lionel: a Union Pacific 'City of Portland' three-car diesel unit, c 1934, next to a Mini Scale NYC 'Hudson', c 1937. They are shown with the Lionel 'Hell Gate Bridge'.*

MARBLES

Marbles are long-established collectibles, with the value of top examples now fetching thousands of dollars! Although the majority of marbles are machine-made, the most desirable specimens are handmade.

There are enormous amounts of marbles available but sought-after types include swirls, with variations such as clambroth – a milk glass with multicolored swirls running through the solid base color; Indian swirls – black with twists of brilliant color over the surface; Latticinio swirls – having a 'lacy' center surrounded by swirls; and Lutz marbles – the swirled ball enriched with copper grains (these are known as Goldstone swirls). Other swirl types include 'open core', where the swirl is in the core of the marble; peppermint, where the swirls resemble peppermint candy; 'solid core' swirls,

ABOVE AND BELOW: *A sample of the vast range of marbles available to the collector.*

which are similar to peppermint but in different colors. One variation of the 'core' swirl is the childhood favorite known as 'cat's eye'. Every collector will have his or her special choices.

Other favorite styles include agates or 'aggies', made from stone which is either in its natural color or artificially dyed; clay marbles, used in both the earliest specimens and in modern ones; 'cloud' marbles, made of glass, with a solid core encapsulated in a clear shell; micas, in which the glass marbles incorporate flakes of mica, giving the silvery effect of tiny fish scales; and sulphides, clear glass marbles in which a china figure is embedded.

Marbles, as with most toys (with the exception of teddy bears, where wear and tear – the scars of having been much loved – are acceptable) are valued in pristine condition. Generally, size is also a factor, the rule being the bigger the better.

LUNCH BOXES

These metal boxes from the 1950s and the 1960s, bright with logos and icons of childhood, are among the hottest things in collecting at the moment complete with fast escalating prices. The fact that lunch boxes were turned out in vast quantities is countered by their poor survival rate, a classic situation with many childhood collectibles. Despite their lowly status, these boxes demonstrate a high quality of lithographic printing, acting as a showcase for the work of some of the leading commercial illustrators of the period, such as Robert Burton, Ed Wexler and Nick Lobianco. Although vinyl plastic came into use in 1959, and a new generation of brunch bags, also in vinyl, were introduced for the teenagers who had outgrown their lunch box years, these have few aficionados. The true, all-American lunch box is a simple rec-

tangular or dome-topped lithographed tin, at its best combining the qualities of tin toys and comics. It is part of the national perception of childhood experience and is responsible for an assault of nostalgia. Its best years were the 1950s and 1960s after which metal was mainly usurped by plastic on safety grounds. In those two decades lunch box sales topped 120 million, during which time virtually every character from children's mythology, from Hopalong Cassidy to the Munsters, had been given the ultimate seal of juvenile approval: appearing on a lunch box. But the history of lunch boxes pre-dates the 1950s. From the 19th century until 1950, it had been a simple, utility container, favored by construction and other manual workers. The invention of the vacuum flask in 1913 allowed for beverages or soups to feature on the menu and, in 1921, Aladdin Industries introduced the dome-topped lunch box, the lid of which could accommodate the flask.

Although Walt Disney had issued a novelty Mickey Mouse school lunch box in 1935, and there were others on the market at about that time, legend has it that the idea of putting a character on a lunch box for children was mooted during a meeting of Aladdin executives looking for a way to boost sales. In any event, the choice of Hopalong Cassidy for their first 'character' box was an inspired one. Within the first year (1950) 600,000 boxes had gone to school. The trend was well and truly set. The rivalry between box manufacturers went into top gear when American Thermos (which later became King Seeley Thermos, a major lunch box company) brought out the Roy Rogers and Dale Evans lunch box, outgunning Hopalong Cassidy with sales of two and a half million in the first year.

Thereafter the wars between these and other producers such as Adco and Ohio Art ensured that new graphics and characters were constantly coming out, though the boxes themselves retained the standard format. Walt Disney characters were only some of the cartoon characters featured on boxes, though they did establish the record for the all-time best-seller, with 'School-bus', featuring a bus load of Disney favorites – nine million boxes!

TOP LEFT: Amongst many Walt Disney lunch boxes, 'School-bus', designed by Al Konetzi for Aladdin, is regarded as the classic with its adaptation of the traditional Workman's dome-topped shape.

LEFT: The Aladdin Workman's lunch box, first introduced in 1921, led a worthy but uneventful existence until it was transformed into a variety of garish pop art school lunch kits.

BELOW: Aladdin's Hopalong Cassidy, introduced in 1950, is credited with popularizing the decorated school lunch box. The illustration was a simple decal, yet it sold 600,000 in its first year.

ABOVE AND BELOW: *Lone Ranger, one of several television Western designs used for lunch boxes.*

ABOVE AND BELOW: *Although television characters dominate lunch-box graphics, sport was portrayed in 'NFL Quarterback', designed by lunch box illustrator Robert Burton for Aladdin Industries, 1964.*

ADULT PLAYTIME COLLECTIBLES

Gambling toys with the spice of dishonesty,
mechanical banks that swallow your
money – games for grownups.

ABOVE: *A cast metal animated bank. These mechanical marvels have a variety of actions by which the coin is deposited into the bank.*

GAMBLING TOYS

From the sophisticated Mississippi riverboat gambler and the smoke-filled Wild West saloon, to the glitz of Las Vegas or Atlantic City, gambling has enjoyed a romantic, exciting image, despite the belief by various sections of the community that it is evil. Some states even ran lotteries in the last century, to raise money for civic projects. Antique lottery tickets are attractive as pieces of rare printed ephemera, as well as for their gambling connection. The same applies to the ephemeral items of horse-racing: posters, postcards, race cards and race-track souvenirs.

On the home or club front, gambling equipment varies from simple dice to such sophisticated items as roulette wheels and slot machines. Dice, which date back to primitive times, were traditionally made of bone or ivory, with plastic a fairly recent introduction. They are especially interesting if they are 'cheaters', loaded to come up on certain numbers.

The spice of dishonesty flavors other gambling collectibles, such as cards, card sharp's equipment, and roulette wheels. Books on gambling, as well as postcards and souvenirs of casinos also fall within the subject.

One of the most familiar gambling devices is the slot machine or 'one-armed bandit', which has become an increasingly popular collectible over

RIGHT: *Wilburs chocolate vendor by the National Vending Machine Co., 1904. Its fragility means few have survived.*

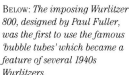

BELOW: *The imposing Wurlitzer 800, designed by Paul Fuller, was the first to use the famous 'bubble tubes' which became a feature of several 1940s Wurlitzers.*

the last few years. The fact that these are gambling devices, however, means that some states make ownership illegal, while others restrict ownership to machines above a certain age. These regulations have caused slot machines to be latecomers to the collectors' market, especially when further tested by horror stories of over-zealous authorities impounding and destroying valuable vintage pieces. Even now, the collector is advised to be sure of the legal position in their area.

The modern slot machine with its spinning wheels was invented by Charles Fey in 1905. By the 1920s several manufacturers were producing machines based on Fey's design. The year 1927 saw the introduction of the jackpot feature, although there were further developments and refinements, such as anti-cheat devices.

These latter are of particular interest, for although there are still people who claim to be able to gauge the 'rhythm' of a machine and pull down the handle at the right moment, the introduction of random timing in the late 1940s ensured that that particular skill is now in the realm of folklore. In the early 1950s electric illumination was added, although the styling of some machines still carried on the opulent traditions of the pre-war era. Numerous small companies have made slot machines but the major manufacturers are Buckley, Mills, Jennings, Pace and Watling.

An interesting adjunct to slot machines is the 'polk' figure. For early 1940s machines, Frank Polk carved lifesized figures from the Old West, such as cowboys and prospectors. The torso incorporated the slot machine, while the handle was supplied by one of the figure's arms. These colorful polk figures were often very detailed. Among the most desirable polk machines are those representing

PINBALLS

There has long been controversy as to whether pinball machines count as games of skill or chance. On one occasion when the issue was before the courts, an expert player consistently achieved higher scores over a novice, thus demonstrating the skill element. Nevertheless, there has always been a gambling element in pinball's history, not only in such obvious mutants as Jennings 'Sportsman' and 'Wall Street' of the 1930s, which were slot machines disguised as pinball tables, but also in the games that paid out cash rewards. In some areas, even games which awarded a 'free play' for a high score were considered gambling devices.

Pinball evolved from the bagatelle game which was popular in the last century. During the 1930s David Gottlieb, who was to become America's largest pinball manufacturer, developed the game of bagatelle into a mechanical, coin-operated device which heralded the modern game.

As with bagatelle, the early pinball games rested on a countertop. Legs were added in 1932. Thereafter, the addition of electricity and the successive appearance of features such as the anti-tilt device (1934), bumpers (1936), 'flippers' (1947), kicking rubbers (1950), and score totalizers (1953) were the major changes, prior to solid state technology in 1977.

Pinball collectors are equally fascinated by the artwork of such manufacturers as Gottlieb, Williams, Bally and United, as well as by the permutation of features which gives each machine its 'personality'. Apart from historical early examples, the fun-value of a game is important. As a pintable takes up considerable space, most collectors want to be able to get some enjoyment out of playing their hobby!

STILL AND MECHANICAL BANKS

Still banks are simply non-animated money boxes. In order to encourage children to save and adults to buy them, they are frequently in a decorative or novelty form. They were also an ideal subject for advertising giveaways or premiums. Quite often candies were sold in a glass or tin container which became a bank when its contents had been consumed.

Although decorative cast-iron banks from the late 19th and early 20th centuries are much prized, age in itself does not set the value. Particularly with figural banks, it is the quality of the model which counts. Some advertising banks are in the shape of the article being promoted or, as in the case of the Sinclair Oil dinosaur, the company's symbol.

the soldiers on either side of the Civil War. These figures came complete with an authentic rifle of the period. Polk figures have been reproduced; some reproductions are close in quality to the originals, while others are mere fiberglass parodies.

While polk figures drew attention to the slot machine, there were others where the contrary effect was desired. This was particularly the case where a machine was being used illegally, and 'baby slots', such as the 1938 'vest pocket' by the Mills Novelty Company or the 1934 Mills QT, were compact enough to be easily removed and hidden if law enforcement officers arrived.

Gambling machines were also overtly disguised – a favorite method was the 'trade stimulator'. These machines, in a wide variety of designs, were particularly popular from the early days of this century to the 1930s. Avoiding the charge of illegal gambling, these machines either paid out a prize – often chewing gum – or a token which was redeemable against merchandise in the store where the machine was located. By tacit understanding, however, the clerk might pay cash out against a winning token! Coin machine tokens, which were mainly used in trade stimulators, but occasionally for jukeboxes and vendors, are much collected. The leading book on this subject lists over 10,000 different tokens, so the variety is enormous.

WORLDS FAIR BANK

TOP LEFT: *Ceramic pig bank for the Rice Sausage Co., 1920s.*

TOP RIGHT: *Novelty slot machine money bank advertising Reno Nevada. Die-cast metal made by Bigler Manufacturing Co. in the 1940s.*

CENTER: *The 'Ideola' musical money bank in molded plastic by Ideal is closely modelled on the Rock-ola juke box of 1947.*

BELOW RIGHT: *Depression era piggy bank counsels saving to 'keep the wolf away'.*

BELOW LEFT: *A die-cast metal slot machine bank, advertising Las Vegas, made by Reno Plastics in the 1940s. This bank features a handle that pulls, spinning reels and a simple jackpot.*

ABOVE: *Molded plastic junior player money bank, dated 1974.*

PUNCHBOARDS

The punchboard was a perforated card, each hole containing a ticket. The face of the board was covered with brightly printed, eye-catching period graphics on paper. Having paid a fee, the player punched a hole through the façade; the ticket thus revealed gave the value of the prize.

It is the colored graphics which give the cards their appeal, and it is this attribute which attracts the knowledgeable collector. But most importantly, the punchboard must be unused, unless there is some compensating factor of age or rarity.

OFFICE COLLECTIBLES

The modern office, a veritable Star Ship Enterprise of electronic communications, is one of the most obvious examples of technological progress. Yet, by substituting Babbidge's adding machine, the forerunner of the computer, nearly all the main ingredients – the telephone, the dictating machine (which developed from Edison's cylinder talking machine) and the typewriter – date back to the last century. In terms of office hardware, the most popular collectible is still the typewriter which, in its modern form – with the letters typed in view of the operator – was invented by John Underwood in 1895.

The first commercially manufactured typewriter was made by E. Remington and Sons and appeared in 1874, although it was not until the turn of the century, following Underwood's invention, that the typewriter came into general use.

Other office collectibles include staplers, pencil sharpeners, inkwells (particularly advertising ones) and pens, which also form a subject in their own right.

LAPEL BUTTONS

Whereas in the past, tramps have been employed to walk around wearing advertising 'sandwich' boards, the button has proved an ideal way for the public to act as unpaid advertising sites. The pinback or lapel button became the successor to the medal-style badge which was popular from the 1880s. Celluloid over tin, paper or thin card over tin, and printed tin were used for these buttons, which appeared early this century.

Extensively used in political campaigns, often with slogans such as the famous 'I like Ike', these buttons, together with other campaign items, also feature as a major section of political collectibles. Buttons have also served as miniature platforms for personal statements on labour, civil rights and women's rights campaigns, as well as promoting

Mechanical banks are usually of cast iron, although tin and, (more recently), plastic have been used. They feature an animated figure or figures which go through actions to deposit the coin in the bank. A much illustrated example is the bank consisting of the head of a large black man. A coin placed in his hand is then transferred into his mouth. Other traditional banks include a tableau of William Tell, a dentist, a kicking mule and a hunter. Many cast-iron novelty mechanical banks have been reproduced, and the novice collector should be familiar with the genuine examples to safeguard against being caught.

LET'S GO WINTHROP BEAT DANVERS Compliments of SEN. QUIGLEY

ELECT COHEN ATT'Y GENERAL

IKE IN '56

STATE SENATOR SCHLOSSTEIN

ELECT GEO. FARNAM STATE SENATOR

ONE ISSUE ONE PLATFORM DANAHER For U.S. Senator RECOVERY

RUSS BOYCE FOR SENATE COMMITTEE 12th DISTRICT

RE-ELECT ZELLER COMPTROLLER

I LIKE IKE

DEWEY WARREN

BILL PURTELL

VOTE STRAIGHT FOR DOWE COMPTROLLER DEMOCRATIC

SADLAK

CHARLES F. HURLEY FOR GOVERNOR

I BELONG TO THE AMERICAN AGRICULTURIST ARMY 150,000 STRONG

ELECT SHANNON GOVERNOR

WIN WITH MIM FOR U.S. CONGRESS E. Q. DADDARIO

COLLINS FOR CONGRESS

RE-ELECT SADLAK CONG. AT LARGE

Re-Elect SADLAK CONGRESSMAN AT LARGE

THE PEOPLE'S CHOICE CONTE

Top: *An array of typical political lapel buttons. The Eisenhower 'I like Ike' campaign produced one of the most famous slogans ever.*

STATE OF OHIO

LIEUTENANT

Left and facing page, top: *As the prime symbol of the service, badges are prized examples of police collectibles. Beware of reproductions appearing on the market.*

Facing page, Below left: *Pinback badge depicting a fireman rescuing an infant from a burning building, c 1880.*

Facing page, Below right: *Badge from the Departments of Correction, State of Alabama.*

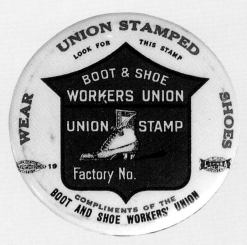

TOP LEFT: *The moon landing celebrated in a commemorative badge.*

TOP RIGHT: *Buttons have advertised virtually everything from commercial products such as coffee to labor rights, as with this button for the Boot and Shoe Workers Union.*

BELOW LEFT: *The original owner of this badge took the advice of the manufacturer, the Whitehead and Hoag Co., and kept it in its envelope, which accounts for its pristine condition.*

BELOW RIGHT: *The early fire services produced magnificent medallions such as this one, which would have been worn with pride at parades. This example was issued for the New England Field Day, 12 September 1895.*

LEFT: *The humble button is given an air of dignity with this patriotic image. Patriotic items are in themselves highly collectible.*

advertisers were Goodrich, Ives, Eveready Batteries, Lucky Strike Cigarettes and Happiness Candy. Sponsorship brought shows by the 'Cliqust Club Eskimos', the 'Gold Dust Twins', and the 'A & P Gypsies', soon joined by the 'Ampico Hour', and the 'Atwater Kent Hour'. In 1928 Pepsodent Toothpaste began its legendary association with the 'Amos 'n' Andy Show'.

By the 1930s and 1940s, the cult of the radio reached its peak in sets which were actually designed to represent particular products. Examples included the Champion Sparkplug, Coca-Cola and Pepsi-Cola bottle-shaped radios, Coca-Cola dispenser-chest-shaped radios and character radios immortalizing Disney characters, the ventriloquist's dummy Charlie McCarthy, Hopalong Cassidy, and the Lone Ranger.

TELEVISION SETS

The earliest surviving television sets were the product of the 1920s and early 1930s. These 'mechanical' prototypes are considered, for reasons of their great scarcity and rarity, to be outside the scope of collectibles. Their successors, the first electric sets, represent the true beginning of the television age. By the years preceding World War II, radio had alerted investors to the potential of the newer medium.

In 1935, RCA, announced the commital of $1,000,000 to television demonstrations, and by 1940 over 10,000 sets were on the market. On 30 April, 1939, Franklin D. Roosevelt became the first president to appear on the gray flickering screen. The next month saw a single camera record the first televised baseball game – Princeton versus Columbia. The next televised game – between the Brooklyn Dodgers and the Cincinnati Reds – used two cameras, and throughout the year, outside broadcasts covered other sporting events, as well as the premier of *Gone with the Wind*.

Studio productions included drama and cookery demonstrations; due to the hot lights, the latter had to be confined to salads! By 1940 there were 23 television stations. After 1945, a highly-developed electronics industry and the first stirrings of the 'consumer society' combined to catapult the public into a new world, in which television became a social and cultural arbiter of taste. By the end of the 1940s Ed Sullivan was broadcasting his first shows. In 1951 came 'I Love Lucy' and 'Dragnet', the cult shows which were to dominate the 1950s. Top collectors' television sets of the postwar peroid include the rare, short-lived CBS rotating wheel color set of 1946, and the Philco Corporation Predicta set of 1958. Portable sets of the late 1950s are now attracting attention for their period styling.

virtually everything from the Mickey Mouse Club and film and pop star fan club to fast foods, exhibitions, leisure parks and other tourist attractions.

Popular slogans emanating from TV and radio shows started the craze for buttons bearing enigmatic messages; this reached a peak during the 1970s, by which time button enthusiasts were all but covering themselves with multicolored scales composed of slogans, pictures and symbols.

RADIO ADVERTISING

During the early days of radio, the big question was: How would broadcasting stations derive an income? In 1922 *Radio Broadcast* magazine put forward various ideas, including that philanthropic millionaires could finance broadcasting in the same way that Andrew Carnegie had given money to libraries and the arts. Finance from government, with revenue produced through a tax on radios was another proposal. In the event, the decision went quite another way. Radio and marketing history was made on 28 August 1922, with the first radio commercial. This promoted the Queensboro's sale of apartments in Jackson Heights, Long Island.

The next stage in the history of radio marketing occurred in January 1923, when the actress Marion Davies made a broadcast sponsored by the cosmetic company Mineralava, entitled 'How I make up for the movies'. Listeners were invited to write in for an autographed photo, and the response to this, the first radio premium, convinced the advertising industry of radio's exploitative value. Pioneer

BIBLIOGRAPHY

S. Applebaum, *The New York World's Fair 1939–40*. Dover Publications 1977.

Plasticville: Market Price Guide. April Publications Inc. 1982.

John Axe, *Collectible Black Dolls*. Hobby House Press 1978.

John Axe, *The Encyclopedia of Celebrity Dolls*. Hobby House Press 1983.

Barbara Bader, *American Picture Books from Noah's Ark to the Beast Within*. Macmillan 1976.

Stanley L. Baker, *Railroad Collectibles: An Illustrated Value Guide*. Collector Books 1985.

Paul Baumann, *Collecting Antique Marbles*. Wallace-Homestead 1981.

Stephen Becker, *Comic Art in America*. Simon and Schuster 1959.

Dr James Beckett, *The Official 1988 Price Guide to Baseball Cards*. House of Collectibles 1987.

Dr James Beckett and Dennis W. Eckes, *The Sport, Americana, Baseball Memorabilia and Autograph Price Guide*. Edgewater Book Co. 1985.

Hugh Cleveland, *Bottle Pricing Guide*. Collector Books 1980.

Herbert R. Collins, *Threads of History*. (Political and campaign items.)

Jo Cunningham, *The Collectors' Encyclopedia of American Dinnerware*. Collector Books, 1982.

William C. Darrah, *The World of Stereographs*. Privately printed 1977.

L. R. Docks, *1915–1965 American Premium Record Guide*. Books Americana 1982.

Harold Evans, *Front Page History*. Salem House 1984.

Richard Fitz, *The Official Price Guide to Collectible Toys*. House of Collectibles 1987.

Gene Florence, *The Collector's Encyclopedia of Depression Glass*. Collector Books 1986.

Helmut and Alison Gernsheim, *Photography*. Oxford University Press.

Walter Gibson, *Family Games America Plays*. Doubleday and Co. 1970.

Tony Goodstone, *The Pulps*. Chelsea House 1980.

Greenberg Publishing Co. publish a number of guides to toy trains; authors Bruce C. and Linda F. Greenberg et al.

Grinder and Fathauer, *Radio Collector's Director and Price Guide*. Ironwood Press 1982.

Frank Gruber, *The Pulp Jungle*. Sherbourne Press 1967.

Helene Guarnaccia, *Salt and Pepper Shakers*. Collector Books 1985.

Leslie Halliwell, *The Filmgoer's Companion*. Avon 1978.

Kevin Hancer, *Collectors' Guide to Edgar Rice Burroughs*. Crimson Cutlass 1987.

Linda Hannas, *The Jigsaw Book*. Dial Press 1981.

Marjorie M. and Donald L. Hinds, *Magazine Magic*. The Messenger Book Press 1972.

Louis Holman, *Rose O'Neill Kewpies and Other Works*. Privately printed 1983.

Sharon and Bob Huxford, *The Collectors' Encyclopedia of Roseville Pottery*. Collector Books 1980.

David and Betty Johnson, *Antique Radios: Restoration and Price Guide*. Wallace-Homestead 1982.

John M. Kaduck, *Rare and Expensive Postcards: Book Two*. Wallace-Homestead 1979.

Patricia Frantz Kery, *Great Magazine Covers of the World*. Anbeyville Press 1982.

T. Kitahara, *Cars: Tin Toy Dreams*. Chronicle Books 1985. (Also other publications by Kitahara.)

Ray Klug, *Antique Advertising Encyclopedia*. LW Promotions 1978.

Ralph and Terry Kovel, *The Kovel's Bottle Price List*. Crown, 1984.

Martha K. Krebs, *Advertising Paper Dolls: A Guide for Collectors* (two volumes). Privately printed 1975.

Kurt Krueger, *Meet Me in St Louis: The Exonumia of the 1904 World's Fair*. Krause Publications 1979.

Bessie M. Lindsey, *American Historical Glass*. Charles E. Tuttle 1967.

David Longest, *Character Museum of Cartoon Art: The Story of America in Cartoons*. 1976.

Richard Luckin, *Dining on Rails*. Privately printed 1983.

Morgan McMahon, *A Flick of the Switch*. Vintage Radio 1975.

Jim and Cathy McQuary, *Collectors' Guide to Advertising Cards*. LW Promotions 1975.

Donald Muetin and Robert Hawkins, *The Pinball Reference Guide*. The Mead Co.

Murray Card International, *Catalogue of Cigarette and Other Trade Cards*. Murray Cards International 1983.

Betty Newbound, *The Gunshot Guide to Values of American Made China and Pottery: Book Two*. Privately printed 1983.

Richard O'Brien, *Collecting Toys*. Books Americana 1985.

Keith Osbourne and Brian Pipe, *The International Book of Beer Labels, Mats and Coasters*. Chartwell Books 1979.

Robert M. Overstreet, *The Comic Price Guide*. Privately printed 1983.

Susan Paris and Carol Manos, *The World of Barbie Dolls*. Collector Books 1983.

Christopher Pearce, *Vintage Jukeboxes: The Hall of Fame*. Chartwell Books 1988.

Allan Petretti, *Petretti's Coca-Cola Collectibles Price Guide*. Nostalgia Publications Inc. 1982.

Roger Pribbenow and Jim Lehmann, *Gumball Guide*. Privately printed.

Daniel B. Priest, *American Sheet Music with Prices*. Wallace-Homestead.

Robert H. Rankin, *Official 1982 Price Guide to Military Collectibles*. House of Collectibles 1982.

Richard D. and Barbara Reddock, *Price Guide to Antique Slot Machines*. Wallace-Homestead 1981.

Dawn Reno, *Collecting Black Americana*. Crown Publishing Co. 1986.

Floyd and Marion Rinhalt, *American Minature Case Art*. A. S. Barnes and Co. Inc.

Jerry Robinson, *The Comics: An Illustrated History of Comic Strip Art*. G. P. Putnam 1974.

Dorothy B. Ryan, *Picture Postcards in the United States 1893–1918*. Clarkson N. Potter.

Francene and Louis Sabin, *The One, the Only, the Original Jigsaw Puzzle Book*. Henry Regnery Co., Chicago 1977.

John Salkin and Lauri Gordon, *Orange Crate Art: The Story of Labels that Launched a Golden Era*. Warner Books 1976.

INDEX